REAL SIMPLE

cleaning

Written by KATHLEEN SQUIRES

Photographs by MONICA BUCK

Prop styling by PHILIPPA BRATHWAITE

REAL SIMPLE · Time HOME ENTERTAINMENT

Clean is a relative term, and thank heavens for that. Imagine how unappealing the world would be if we were all held to the same strict standard of clean: spotless sinks, sparkling mirrors, not a dust bunny in sight. Life would feel like an extended stay in a good hotel, which is fun (especially if someone else is making your bed), but certainly not real. Where is the soul? A little dirt by the front door may irritate you to no end, but it's a nice reminder that someone in the house has spent some time outside, hopefully playing baseball or tossing the dog a stick.

Because one person's spick-and-span is another's squalor, we all have different ideas about how much we need to clean. Readers of *Real Simple* magazine frequently tell us editors about their love-hate relationship with the concept. I'm happy to report that there are some hearty, creative souls who make cleaning an event; they put on headphones, dance around the house

(literally), and celebrate afterward with a glass of wine. As you might imagine, these people are

the minority. But even those who hate the process love the results.

Just as there are manifold attitudes toward cleaning, there are manifold systems to tackle it.

Whether you want to cover just the basics (floors, windows) or spend hours on every nook (inside

the oven, anyone?), this book has a cleaning strategy for you. All of us at *Real Simple* know there

is more to life than scrubbing a toilet. Still, there is something redemptive about cleaning: It

promises a fresh start. When life is a mess, you can always clean, and your outlook (not to

mention your house) will be improved. In other words, you can rise above it all—*and* shine. ∎

Kristin van Ogtrop
Managing Editor, *Real Simple*

Contents

Cleaning Kit

Imagine a cleaning challenge looming so large that you're forced to take matters into your own hands. Consider the plight of janitor James Murray Spangler, who, in 1907, was sick of the dust rising as he swept floors. So he mounted an old fan motor to the back of a tin soap box and attached a broom handle to the box. His invention: the vacuum cleaner. A hundred years and a Swiffer later, there's a gizmo on the shelf for nearly every cleaning problem, most promising to work miracles while you lift nary a finger. But which tools really work? And which do you really need? Turns out, you need only the following 20 products to clean your entire place. And, yes, a vacuum is one of them.

1. Microfiber Cloths

Why you need them: Their absorbent nylon fibers attract 99.9 percent of bacteria, according to industry tests. The machine-washable cloths handle nearly any chore.

What to look for: Five cloths in various colors. Designate different colors for different rooms so that your blue cloth, say, is always used in the bathroom.

2. Toilet Brush

Why you need it: The most dreaded of chores requires a tool to be used for it and it alone.

What to look for: A long wand keeps your hand-to-bowl contact minimal. Nonabsorbent nylon bristles repel germs and won't scratch porcelain like those composed of metal wire. A companion caddy helps keep germs contained.

3. Scrub Brush

Why you need it: Burned food in your oven, soot in your fireplace, and mildew-ridden tile require serious scouring.

What to look for: Heavy-duty nylon bristles are the least likely to scratch surfaces. A comfortable handle—rubber is ideal—keeps your skin from coming into contact with abrasive cleansers.

4. Spray Bottle

Why you need it: The bottle comes in handy for spraying homemade stain-removal solutions onto carpets and upholstery. Plus, it makes rinsing large surfaces, such as tubs, easy; just spritz and wipe.

What to look for: Anything goes. Repurpose a drained glass-cleaner container, or buy a plastic bottle at the drugstore.

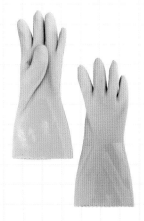

5. Rubber Gloves

Why you need them: Your skin needs protection from certain cleaning agents, especially the chemicals in oven cleaner.

What to look for: Gloves advertised as slim fitting and contoured to the hands. Both traits make it easier to grip tools. A foam lining will absorb interior dampness better than a cotton one will.

6. Toothbrush

Why you need it: The tiny head of a nylon-bristle toothbrush fits into tons of tough-to-reach spots throughout the house—between showerhead holes, around oven handles, and under toilet hinges.

What to look for: Any soft-bristle model you've retired will work, whether it's an electric one or the old-fashioned kind.

**DON'T MIX
THESE PRODUCTS**

For a clean bill of health, avoid these toxic combos.

Rust remover and all-purpose cleaner: When paired with the oxidizing agents in the cleaner, the acid-based rust remover, which contains sodium hydrosulfite, releases sulfur dioxide, a pungent gas that irritates the eyes and the nose.

Tile cleaner with bleach and all-purpose cleaner: Ammonia-based cleaners emit noxious gases when coupled with the sodium hypochlorite ingredient in bleach. Wheezing and coughing ensue.

Dishwashing liquid containing ammonia and automatic-dishwasher detergent: Adding a squirt of dish soap when the gel runs low isn't a smart shortcut. The ammonia in the soap and the bleach in the gel create toxic fumes.

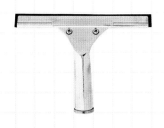

7. Dry-Cleaning Sponge

Why you need it: The tiny pores in this cellulose foam-latex pad attract soot, dust, and pet hair from upholstery, lamp shades, and acoustic tiles without chemicals.

What to look for: Size matters. Find one that's roughly three by six inches so that it fits snugly in your hand but still covers a substantial swath of surface.

8. Squeegee

Why you need it: A professional-grade squeegee has a durable rubber edge that displaces liquid on glass without streaks. It works on mirrors and shower doors, too.

What to look for: Squeegees in sizes similar to your windows. Measure them and pick a squeegee or two with like widths. Fewer strokes equal fewer streaks.

9. Broom

Why you need it: For fireplaces and floors tracked with crumbs, nothing else comes close.

What to look for: Bristles made of nylon catch dirt best, and an angled head can drag the dregs from corners. A lightweight handle eases the strain that sweeping places on shoulders. Look for a broom with a matching dustpan.

10. Sponge Mop

Why you need it: A porous sponge mop can eliminate mud puddles *and* petrified particles.

What to look for: Sponges about 10 inches wide and four inches deep drink more liquid and cover more ground. A chrome handle won't rust, and a plastic wringer lever lets you release liquid without getting your hands wet.

11. Disinfecting Wipes

Why you need them: These towelettes mop up messes in a flash while killing 99.9 percent of bacteria, according to industry tests.

What to look for: Read the fine print on the label. If the product has a registration number from the Environmental Protection Agency (EPA), then it has been proven to kill bacteria, fungi, and viruses.

12. Mild Abrasive

Why you need it: Small mineral or metal granules in the cleanser help you scour scum on tubs and tile with less elbow grease.

What to look for: A chlorine-free creamy cleanser labeled fine for acrylics and fiberglass. Look for the industry-regulated terms "mild" and "gentle," which mean that the soap is safe for most surfaces.

13. Dust Mop

Why you need it: Recent research has shown that the average home can collect up to nine pounds of dust a year on floors. *Nine pounds.*

What to look for: Washable cloth heads made of cotton or micro-fiber attract dirt, hair, and dust. Choose a mop with a long, flexible handle to reach areas above or beyond your arm length.

14. Extendable Duster

Why you need it: Who wants to rig up a ladder just to whisk cobwebs from the ceiling?

What to look for: A removable and extremely durable lamb's-wool head contains the natural chemical lanolin, which attracts and traps dust. A pivoting head can lock into different positions for easier access to corners.

15. White Vinegar

Why you need it: The acetic acid in vinegar cuts through mineral deposits on faucets and windows.

What to look for: Plain distilled white vinegar (not cider, balsamic, or white wine) with a solution of 5 percent acetic acid, just strong enough to do its job. Typically, distilled white vinegar contains 4 to 7 percent acidity.

16. Dishwashing Liquid

Why you need it: You name it, this dirt-cheap liquid cleans it.

What to look for: Scan the label for the industry-regulated words "mild" and "gentle." Artificial coloring rarely stains surfaces, but a clear liquid is safest. You can skip antibacterial formulas—they'll rid your hands, but not your countertops, of germs.

MAKING THEM LAST
The secret to a long life for your supplies? A few preventive measures.
Dust mop: Throw cloths in the washer, but skip the bleach (which damages fibers) and the fabric softener (which eliminates static electricity).
Gloves: Soak gloves in a solution of one part vinegar to three parts warm water to kill germs.
Sponge mop: After each use, soak the head in a bucket of one gallon of water and 3/4 cup of bleach for five minutes so mold spores can't grow. Wring it out well.
Squeegee: Drench a rag in a mixture of half white vinegar and half water and swipe it across the blade to remove residue.
Vacuum: Use a seam ripper (available at craft stores) to pull hair from the rotating brush (on the bottom of upright and canister models).

17. Vacuum

Why you need it: Carpets, curtains, and upholstery get dusty.
What to look for: Strong suction. (Brands are rated by the Carpet and Rug Institute at www.carpet-rug.com.) Choose one with a dust brush and upholstery and crevice attachments. A HEPA (high efficiency particulate air) filter picks up allergens 0.1 micron in size.

18. All-Purpose Cleaner

Why you need it: This spray cuts grease, loosens soil, and leaves behind an invisible coating that prevents dirt from redepositing.
What to look for: A label should include two things: the industry-regulated words "degreaser" or "cuts grease" and an EPA registration number noting that the product is a proven disinfectant.

19. Baking Soda

Why you need it: In its pure form, baking soda (alias: sodium bicarbonate) is a scouring powder. And here's a chemistry lesson: It neutralizes acids and bases, so it eliminates sour-smelling odors instead of covering them up.
What to look for: Be sure the label touts "pure baking soda" or "100 percent sodium bicarbonate."

20. Caddy

Why you need it: When cleaning products are in one place, they're easier to cart from room to room.
What to look for: A sturdy basket or plastic bucket wide enough to fit your cleaners and deep enough to contain spills. Extra credit: Wear a tool apron, and stash your toothbrush, cloths, and dry-cleaning sponge in the pockets.

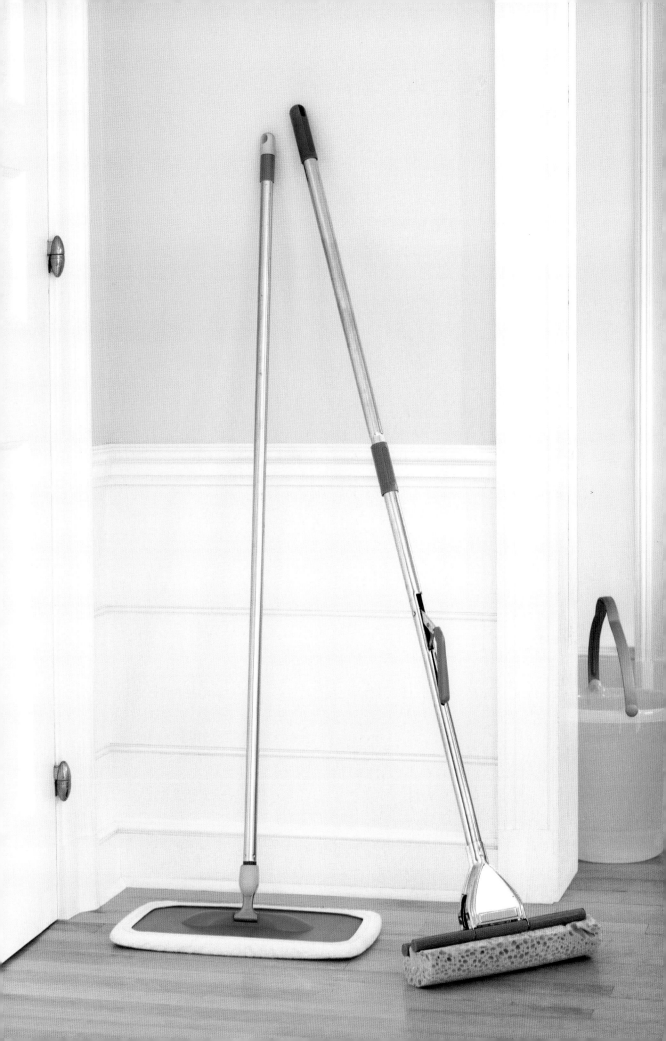

Room by Room

Auntie Em must have kept a clean house. Otherwise, Dorothy would have clicked her ruby slippers and said, "There's no place like a five-star hotel with housekeeping." Because after a long journey—or a long day—no one wants to return to a mess (especially when brooms conjure memories of one wicked witch). To make your home a place you want to come back to, follow this advice for cleaning every space, from the kitchen to the laundry room. You may not be able to stop the tornado, but at least you can tidy up after it.

Kitchen

Between raw-meat drippings and unwashed produce on your countertops, the kitchen tends to be a catchall for a host of bacteria. (*Staphylococcus aureus,* anyone?) And often the dirtiest spots lurk behind closed cabinet doors, under oven-exhaust grates, and inside the dishwasher. Luckily, much the way you prepare your favorite dish, you can whip up a pristine kitchen in a short amount of time by following a carefully tested recipe. Tackling appliances, surfaces, storage areas, and the floor with a simple step-by-step plan and the right cleaning tools makes the decidedly daunting job easier than, say, producing a perfect soufflé. The finished product: floors (and countertops and sinks) you could safely eat off. ▪

Kitchen Cleaning 101

These basic steps will give maximum shine to all your kitchen surfaces with minimal effort and time. Consider the following your starter course.

Step 1: Going in the direction of the grain, wipe cabinet fronts from top to bottom with a microfiber cloth dampened with water and a few drops of mild cleaner. (See Cleaning Your Cabinets and Drawers, page 37, for the right cleaners.) Rinse the cloth, wring it out well, and repeat without the cleaner, taking care to remove cleaner residue that can dull the finish.

Step 2: Wipe the stovetop with a microfiber cloth moistened with water and cleaner. (See Cleaning Your Oven, page 33, for cleaners.)

Step 3: Wet a microfiber cloth with water and mild cleaner and wipe the countertops in a circular motion. (See Cleaning Your Counters, page 23, for cleaners.) To get rid of the soapy film, mist the entire area with water from a spray bottle and wipe it down again with a clean cloth. Wash the tile backsplash using the same method, scrubbing any food splatters from the grout.

Step 4: Wipe the outsides of the refrigerator, the dishwasher, and the microwave. (See Cleaning Kitchen Accessories, page 38.)

Step 5: Disinfect the garbage can by spraying all-purpose cleaner on both the inside and the outside of the bin and wiping it with a clean cloth.

Step 6: With a cloth and cleaner, scrub the sink basin in a circular motion from the top to the drain. (See Cleaning Your Sink, page 27, for cleaners.) Use a toothbrush to remove any mold lurking in the edges of the drain and the faucet. Rinse the entire area with water and wipe it down with a clean cloth to bring out its shine.

Step 7: Sweep the floor with a broom using long strokes and working from the walls to the middle of the room. Try not to lift up the broom at the end of each stroke or dust will be kicked into the air. Make several piles of debris as you go, picking them up with a dustpan and dumping them in the garbage. To clean corners, blow out the dust with a hair dryer, then sweep up. Or vacuum using a crevice attachment to reach tight spots and underneath cabinet bases.

THE 10-MINUTE CLEAN

Impromptu dinner party? Guests tend to congregate in the kitchen. After all, that's where the food and the drinks originate. You can make yours shine in minutes with these steps, listed in order of importance.

- Clean the sink.
- Wipe spills off the stovetop.
- Wipe the counters.
- Sweep up major dust bunnies and debris.
- Wipe the appliances—refrigerator, microwave, oven—concentrating on the handles.

Kitchen Cleaning: Next Steps

Have a little more time on your rubber-gloved hands? Add these seven steps, plus an extra hour or two, to get into all the nooks and crannies.

Step 1: Soak the dish rack, whether it's wooden or stainless steel, in a sink filled with water and a dollop of dishwashing liquid. When the food particles are loosened, scrub them off with a toothbrush. Dry with a clean cloth.

Step 2: Empty cabinets and drawers and vacuum crumbs with a brush attachment. Wipe shelves with a cloth dampened with water and dish soap.

Step 3: Wipe down the inside of the refrigerator. (See Cleaning Your Freezer and Refrigerator, page 31, for techniques.) Move the refrigerator and vacuum behind and underneath.

Step 4: Clean small appliances, such as the coffeemaker, the food processor, and the can opener. (See Cleaning Kitchen Accessories, page 38, for methods.)

Step 5: Clean the oven, using the techniques on page 33. When you're finished, wipe down the oven's door, hardware, and handles.

Step 6: Remove the burner grates from the stovetop and scrub them with a brush and cleaner. (See Cleaning Your Stovetop, page 35, for methods.)

Step 7: Mop the floor in small sections, dipping the mop into a pail of clean water and squeezing out excess liquid in between each section. (Use the cleaners suggested in Floors, page 93.)

And for Extra Credit

EVERY MONTH
- Wipe down the moldings. (For methods, see page 85.)
- Wipe down the walls and the switch plates. (See page 85.)

EVERY THREE MONTHS
- Clean and degrease the stove's hood. (See page 35.)

EVERY SIX MONTHS
- Sweep the corners of the ceiling. (For techniques, see page 83.)
- Vacuum or dust the refrigerator condenser coils. (See page 31.)

EVERY YEAR
- Rid the pantry of expired food and wipe the shelves.

Cleaning Your Counters

Here's a little counter intelligence: Wiping these areas after meals can cut deep-cleaning time in half. Scan to your counter type for the needed steps.

Butcher Block

- Moisten a cloth with white vinegar and wipe down the surface. The acetic acid in the vinegar disinfects by killing lingering bacteria.
- Wet a cloth with warm water and a few drops of dishwashing liquid. Wring it out well and wipe the surface, going with the grain.
- Mist the block with plain water and wipe away soap residue.
- Pat dry with a clean cloth. If the wood gets too wet, it could split or warp.

Linoleum

- Rub the surface in circular strokes, using a cloth spritzed with all-purpose cleaner. Do not use ammonia, which can discolor the finish.
- Dry with a clean cloth.

Plastic Laminate (Such as Formica and Wilsonart)

- Lightly spritz all-purpose cleaner on a moist sponge, cloth, or soft nylon pad and rub in circular strokes. Liquid can seep into the seams and warp the laminate, so wipe gently near the edges. Avoid using abrasive cleansers, steel wool, and stiff-bristle brushes, which can scratch the surface.
- Wipe the surface again with a clean, damp cloth to rinse off the cleaner.

Soapstone

- Dip a cloth or a sponge in warm water with a few drops of dishwashing liquid in it, wring the cloth out, and wipe the surface in circular strokes. Avoid using abrasive cleansers, which can scratch the surface, and ammonia or nonchlorine bleach, which can dry it out.
- Rub mineral oil onto the surface with a cloth every few weeks during the first year (and every two months afterward) to help the stone darken evenly.

Solid Surfaces (Such as Avonite and Corian)

HIGH-GLOSS FINISH

- Dip a cloth in a mixture of one part white vinegar to one part warm water. Wring it out and wipe down the counter in a circular motion.
- Buff dry with a clean cloth.

PROTECTING YOUR COUNTERS

Between hot pots and heavy appliances that get constantly shifted around, your countertops take a beating. Ward off wear and tear with these tips.

- Place small appliances on nonstick silicone baking mats. The mats slide around easily and stop appliance legs from gouging counters.
- Let a marble pastry board double as a trivet so that hot pots don't burn the surface.
- Line counters with parchment paper whenever you're working with foods like lemons and oranges, which contain acids that can discolor the surface.
- When possible, affix appliances, such as a TV, to the underside of cabinets, instead of resting them on the counter.
- Choose medium- to dark-colored grout for ceramic countertops; it hides stains better.
- Apply a light coat of clear furniture wax to laminate counters to repel stains.

Cleaning Your Counters (continued)

Solid Surfaces (Such as Avonite and Corian)

MATTE AND SATIN FINISHES

■ Dampen a cloth with water and a squirt of dishwashing liquid, wring it out well, and wipe the counter in a circular motion. Even if your counter is white, avoid products that contain bleach, which can make the finish appear smoky.

■ Buff dry with a clean cloth.

Stainless Steel

■ Wet a cloth with warm water and a few drops of dishwashing liquid. Don't use ammonia or bleach, which can dull the steel, or abrasive sponges, pads, and cleansers, which can scratch it.

■ Rub with the grain of the surface to lift dirt.

■ Blot dry with a clean towel or cloth; allowing water to evaporate naturally can cause water deposits.

■ Apply a thin layer of stainless-steel polish according to the package instructions, wiping off any excess immediately.

■ Buff the polish onto the stainless-steel counter, always going with the grain, using a clean, dry towel or cloth.

Stone (Granite, Limestone, and Marble)

■ Follow the steps for soapstone (see previous page), omitting the mineral oil.

Tile

GLAZED CERAMIC

■ Mix one capful of rubbing alcohol with one gallon of water and dip a cloth into the solution. Wipe down the surface in a circular motion. Avoid using oil soaps or ammonia, which can yellow grout. Also avoid using vinegar, since its acidity can damage grout.

■ Scrub grout, if necessary, with a toothbrush dipped in the alcohol solution.

UNGLAZED

■ Dilute a few squirts of dishwashing liquid into a gallon of warm water and wet a cloth in the solution. Wipe down the surface in a circular motion.

■ Scrub grout with a toothbrush wet with the dishwashing-liquid solution.

(To find out how to remove stains from these surfaces, see Stains, page 100.)

(To find out how to remove stains from these surfaces, see Stains, page 100.)

WHAT'S *REALLY* ON YOUR COUNTER

Your countertops can play host to a cocktail party of unsavory germs and pests. Next time you tire of scrubbing and disinfecting, remember the two most common kinds of kitchen-counter bacteria that you're wiping out. **Food-borne bacteria:** Salmonella and E. coli don't simply disappear over time if not properly cleaned up. They can survive on countertops and contaminate other food as long as there is moisture to feed them. Avoid infection by washing your counters with dishwashing liquid and hot water before and after handling raw meat and vegetables. **Bug-borne bacteria:** Capable of transmitting 250 diseases to humans, houseflies spit stomach content containing bacteria and viruses they've picked up from pet droppings and other decaying matter, like garbage. They flock to liquids, so keep food covered with plastic wrap while it's on a countertop.

Cleaning Your Sink

After sending murky mop water down the drain, the least you can do for this kitchen workhorse, no matter its finish, is to give it a nice, long rubdown.

Ceramic and Stone (Granite, Limestone, and Marble)

▪ Wet a cloth with warm water, wring it out, and apply a few drops of dishwashing liquid. Rub in a circular motion from the top of the sink to the drain. On stone surfaces, avoid abrasive cleansers, which can scratch the surface; ammonia and bleach products, which can dull the finish; and vinegar- and lemon-based cleansers, which can eat through stone.
▪ Spray the entire surface with water and wipe down with a clean cloth.

Porcelain Enamel

▪ Spritz a cloth with all-purpose cleaner and wipe down the sink from the top to the drain. Or use this time-saving tip: Fill the sink to the brim with warm water and toss in a few denture-cleaning tablets. The chemicals in the tablets will cut stains. Never use abrasive pads, cleansers, or wire-bristle brushes, which can scratch the finish.
▪ Spray the entire surface with water and wipe down with a clean cloth.

Solid Surfaces (Such as Avonite and Corian)

HIGH-GLOSS FINISH

▪ Dip a cloth in a mixture of one part white vinegar and one part water and wipe down the sink from top to bottom in a circular motion.

MATTE AND SATIN FINISHES

▪ Dampen a cloth with water and a squirt of dishwashing liquid. Wipe down the sink using the same technique for a high-gloss finish. Avoid products with bleach, which can leave spots.

Stainless Steel

▪ Wet a cloth with warm water and a few drops of dishwashing liquid. Rub with the grain to lift dirt. Don't use ammonia or bleach, which can dull steel, or abrasive sponges and cleansers, which can scratch it.
▪ Blot dry; allowing water to evaporate naturally can cause water deposits.
▪ Apply a thin layer of stainless-steel polish according to the package instructions, wiping off any excess.
▪ Buff the polish onto the steel with a clean, dry cloth, going with the grain.

(To learn how to remove stains from these surfaces, see Stains, page 100.)

SINK STOPPED UP?

Here's how to get things moving again.

If your drain is clogged:
▪ Pour 1/2 cup of baking soda down the drain. (It's best not to use chemicals, which can corrode pipes and may harm septic systems.)
▪ Slowly pour down 1/2 cup of white vinegar. Wait for it to foam.
▪ Cover the drain with a stopper and let the solution sit for five minutes.
▪ Flush the drain with a gallon of boiling water.

If your garbage disposal is clogged:
▪ First, try running hot water for a few minutes to dislodge food en route to the drain. That often cures minor clogs.
▪ Turn on the disposal. If it is noisier than usual or hums but the blades don't turn, the disposal is probably still clogged.
▪ Turn off the power from the fuse box or circuit breaker.
▪ Use a wooden spoon to clear stubborn food. Never use your fingers, as the blades are sharp.
▪ Turn on the power. No change? Call a plumber.

Cleaning Your Faucets and Fixtures

On tap: brilliant ways to shine every kind of spigot. The key for all is to avoid ammonia, steel wool, and abrasive pads, which can strip or scratch the finish.

Brass

- Apply dishwashing liquid to a damp cloth and wipe down the faucet.
- Use a cotton swab to clean the edges and the mounting. Dental floss can break up hardened deposits in crevices.
- If your fixture is unlacquered, polish it by smoothing brass cream onto a cloth and rubbing the fixture. (Dab a bit of polish onto an inconspicuous spot with a white cloth. If the cloth turns black, the faucet is unlacquered.)
- Wipe with a water-spritzed cloth and dry with a clean cloth.

Bronze and Gold Plated

- Follow the instructions above, omitting the brass cream.

Chrome

- Spray the faucet with water and wipe it down with a cloth, using a cotton swab or dental floss to clean the edges and the mounting.
- For extra shine, spray glass cleaner onto a cloth and wipe the faucet.

Copper

- Apply dishwashing liquid to a damp cloth and wipe down the faucet, using cotton swabs or dental floss to clean the edges and the mounting.
- Apply a commercial copper polish (available at hardware stores) to a soft cloth and rub the faucet, following the package instructions.

Nickel

- Wipe water and mineral deposits with a clean, dry cloth to rub them out.
- Use a cotton swab or dental floss to clean the edges and the mounting.
- Spray glass cleaner onto a cloth and wipe the fixture, then let it air-dry.

Stainless Steel

- Wet a cloth with warm water and a few drops of dishwashing liquid, then rub the fixture to lift dirt.
- Blot dry with a clean cloth to prevent water deposits from forming.
- Apply a thin layer of stainless-steel polish according to the package instructions, wiping off any excess immediately.
- Buff the polish onto the faucet with a clean, dry cloth, going with the grain.

WHAT'S IN YOUR WATER?

Your H_2O runs clear, so what is that green gunk you're furiously scrubbing off the faucets? Here's a color code.

Blue green residue: When copper plumbing begins to corrode, blue green residue builds up around faucets. Small doses of copper are safe, but extremely high levels can trigger stomach cramps. So government watchdogs, like the Environmental Protection Agency, set health standards for drinking water. (For more information, go to www.epa.gov/safewater/dwinfo/index.html.)

Reddish orange residue: Iron, a naturally occurring nutrient in water, produces rusty brown stains on plumbing fixtures when it comes into contact with oxygen. It's no cause for concern.

Cleaning Your Freezer and Refrigerator

You may think you have the technique down cold, but cleaning the refrigerator requires more than a box of baking soda. Here's a refresher course.

Interior

- Empty the contents of the freezer, seal them in containers, and place the containers in coolers. Thaw the freezer. (See Defrosting Your Freezer, right.)
- Empty the contents of the refrigerator. Perishable foods generally won't spoil within 30 minutes if they have been refrigerated properly.

CRISPERS AND ICE MAKER

- Fill the sink with warm water (scalding water can crack plastic), adding six tablespoons of dish soap. Wash the crispers and the ice maker. Or put them in the dishwasher. (See Stick This in Your Dishwasher, page 20.)
- Dry with a clean cloth.

DOORS, SHELVES, AND WALLS

- Dip a cloth in a mixture of two tablespoons of baking soda and one quart of warm water. Wipe the walls, the shelves, and the inside of the doors. Use a vacuum with a crevice attachment to remove bits of food in corners.
- Rinse the cloth and wet it with the baking-soda solution. Scrub the door's rubber gaskets with the cloth, reaching into the folds, then wipe dry.

Exterior

CONDENSER COILS

- Use a vacuum and the brush attachment to remove dust stuck to the coils, which are found on the back of the refrigerator or behind the front grill. Vacuum underneath the refrigerator and along the wall to prevent further buildup. (Casters, available at hardware stores, can help you maneuver the mammoth machine.)

DOOR HANDLES

- Wipe with a wet, soapy cloth. Clean joints with a cotton swab.

FIBERGLASS

- Spray all-purpose cleaner onto a cloth and wipe in long, vertical strokes.

STAINLESS STEEL

- Wet a cloth with warm water and a few drops of dishwashing liquid, wring it out well, and rub with the grain to lift dirt. Blot dry.
- Apply a thin layer of stainless-steel polish according to the package instructions, wiping off any excess immediately.
- Buff the polish onto the stainless steel with a clean, dry towel or cloth, going with the grain.

DEFROSTING YOUR FREEZER

Unless your freezer is a newer, self-defrosting one (meaning that a small heat charge surges through the coils once a day, raising the temperature ever so slightly, so that frost doesn't form), you must thaw the freezer's icy walls before sanitizing them. Follow these steps.

- Empty the freezer and unplug the refrigerator.
- Remove the drain plug, a stopper that is connected to a hose on the inside of the freezer.
- Leave the door open and place a bowl of warm water inside the freezer to raise the temperature and help melt the ice.
- Remove the metal grid at the bottom of the refrigerator and place a rimmed baking dish under the drain tube.
- Shave the ice off the walls of the freezer using a nylon spatula (metal can scratch the walls). No need to scoop out the ice—it will melt and drain into the baking dish.

Cleaning Your Oven

A hot spot for grease and charred food, the oven has a complicated list of parts to clean. Warm up with the burners, then move on to the racks inside.

Interior

CONTINUOUS

▪ Wipe spills as soon as possible using a cloth sprayed with a nonabrasive cleaner. Otherwise, since this oven has a special, chemically treated finish that burns off food splatters as they happen, it doesn't require extensive interior cleaning (though it is unable to oxidize large spills). Do not use oven cleaners, powdered cleansers, or abrasives, which damage the finish.

CONVENTIONAL

▪ Remove the racks and side supports and scrub them with dishwashing liquid and water. Use a soft brush or steel wool to remove stubborn particles.

▪ Apply a nonalkaline oven cleaner to the interior, following the package instructions. The lye in some oven cleaners can sear skin, so slip on rubber gloves before spraying on the cleaner.

▪ Wipe the walls with a clean cloth.

SELF-CLEANING

▪ Remove and clean the racks as directed for a conventional oven.

▪ Turn on the cleaning cycle. Its sky-high temperatures will burn spills into an ashy substance. Note: Never use a commercial oven cleaner on the interior, since it can damage the finish.

▪ When the cycle is done, wipe out the ashes with a cloth. Throw them away.

▪ Wipe down the area with a damp cloth.

Exterior

GLASS CERAMIC AND PORCELAIN ENAMEL

▪ Wipe down the oven with a damp cloth and dishwashing liquid. Avoid abrasive sponges, pads, and cleansers, which can easily scratch the surface.

▪ Rinse with a clean, damp cloth and allow the oven to air-dry.

STAINLESS STEEL

▪ Check your manual for instructions, then wet a cloth with warm water and a few drops of dishwashing liquid. Rub the exterior with the grain to lift dirt.

▪ Blot dry with a clean towel to prevent water deposits from forming.

▪ Apply a thin layer of stainless-steel polish according to the package instructions, wiping off any excess immediately.

▪ Buff the polish onto the stainless steel, going with the grain, using a clean, dry towel or microfiber cloth.

AVOIDING FOOD OVERFLOW

Some foods have a habit of breaking boundaries while baking, dripping batter and liquids onto the oven floor. Here's how to handle the worst offenders.

Casseroles: Line the bottom of the oven with aluminum foil. Wad up any spills and throw away the foil.

Custards: Often baked in convection ovens with fans, they need a stay-put foundation. Spritz a baking pan with cooking spray, line it with parchment paper (which sticks to the spray), and set the dish on top.

Muffins: Use a measuring cup with a spout to pour batter into muffin tins neatly, avoiding drips on the tin that can burn and flake off. To cap ballooning muffin tops, never fill the tins more than three-fourths full.

Pies: Sit pie dishes on top of a silicone mat (the kind used for baking cookies) set on a baking sheet. The mat will catch any bubbling fruit that migrates over the edge.

OVEN
TEMPERATURE

REAR

FRONT

OVEN

Dual Fuel
Thermal-Convection
Automatic Re-ignition

Cleaning Your Stovetop

What starts in a sauté pan doesn't always stay there. Clean up oil splatters, marinara drips, and gummy exhaust fans with these top-notch tips.

Cooktop

GLASS CERAMIC AND PORCELAIN ENAMEL

- Wipe the stovetop with a cloth wet with dishwashing liquid and warm water. Avoid abrasive sponges, pads, and cleansers, which can scratch the surface.
- For deeper cleaning, sprinkle baking soda directly onto the surface and rub with a slightly damp cloth. Let the baking soda sit for five minutes.
- Rinse with a clean, damp cloth and allow the surface to air-dry.

STAINLESS STEEL

- Wet a cloth with warm water and a few drops of dishwashing liquid. Rub with the grain to lift dirt.
- Blot dry with a clean towel or cloth to prevent water deposits.
- Apply a thin layer of stainless-steel polish according to the package instructions, wiping off any excess immediately.
- Buff polish onto the cooktop with a clean, dry cloth, going with the grain.

Electric-Burner Coils

- Scrub the coils with a cloth soaked in hot water and dishwashing liquid.

Exhaust Fan

- Vacuum the fan with a brush attachment or dust it with a dust-mop cloth.
- Wipe away grease buildup with all-purpose cleaner applied to a cloth.

Gas-Burner Grates, Knobs, and Handles

- Soak grates, knobs, and handles in hot, soapy water for five minutes. (Knobs can often be placed in the dishwasher. See page 20.)
- With a soft dish brush, flake off food in crevices of grates and on handles.
- Rinse all the parts thoroughly with clean water.
- Dry with a clean cloth. Make sure everything is completely dry before replacing; otherwise, moisture can drip into the oven (from the knobs) or the ignition mechanism (from the grates), causing a malfunction.

Hood and Hood Filter

- Remove the filter and soak it for 10 minutes in hot, soapy water. Meanwhile, wet a cloth with hot, soapy water and wipe down the hood.
- Dry both thoroughly with a clean cloth.

FOUR MORE USES FOR OVEN CLEANER
While it should always be used in ventilated areas (and never on aluminum or chrome), here are four ways to fire up the oven cleaner.

- Spray it on stained Pyrex dishes. Place them inside a tightly sealed garbage bag overnight. In the morning, scrub with a brush. Wash thoroughly.
- Dampen a cloth with the cleaner and wipe sticky product residue off a cool curling iron. Wipe with water before using, since oven cleaner can burn skin.
- Squirt some cleaner onto oil and grease spots on a concrete driveway. Let it work for several minutes, then spray with a high-pressure garden hose.
- Spray sap-covered garden tools and place them in a sealed plastic bag for several minutes. Rinse them thoroughly before reusing.

Cleaning Your Cabinets and Drawers

Whether your cupboards are bare or filled to the gills, you shouldn't have to pry the jelly jar off a sticky foundation. Make cabinets gleam, inside and out.

Interior

- Remove crumbs and grit in corners with a handheld vacuum or a vacuum's crevice attachment. Loosen gooey spills (like honey) with an old credit card.
- Wipe down shelves with a cloth barely dampened with water and dishwashing liquid. Gently scrub any remaining sticky spots with a toothbrush.
- Dry with a cloth as you work; if wood becomes saturated, it may buckle.

Exterior

LAMINATE

- Spray all-purpose cleaner onto a microfiber cloth, wring it out, and wipe down the cabinet fronts in vertical strokes. (For tough grime, spray cleaner directly onto the stain, let stand for two minutes, then wipe. Liquid can seep into seams and damage laminate, so use cleaner sparingly.) Avoid abrasive cleansers and steel wool, which can scratch the surface.
- Wipe down the knobs with the cloth sprayed with all-purpose cleaner.
- Buff with a clean cloth.

STAINLESS STEEL

- Wet a cloth with water and dish soap, wring it out, and wipe with the grain.
- Wipe down the knobs with the cloth.
- Blot dry with a clean cloth to avoid water deposits.
- Apply a thin layer of stainless-steel polish and buff it onto the cabinets and the knobs with a clean, dry cloth, going with the grain.

THERMOFOIL

- Spritz glass cleaner onto a cloth and wipe the cabinets, going with the grain.
- Wipe the knobs with the cloth and glass cleaner.
- Buff dry with a clean cloth.

WOOD

- Going with the grain, wipe the cabinets using a cloth wet with water and wood cleaner or dish soap. Wring out the cloth; excess water can damage wood. (Caution: If your wood is painted, use only dish soap and test a spot. If the color changes, call a paint store to find a cleaner for your paint brand.)
- Rub the cloth gently over the knobs.
- If you have glass-paned cabinets, spray glass cleaner on a crumpled piece of newspaper and wipe in long strokes, from top to bottom.
- Buff the entire cabinet in horizontal strokes with a dry cloth.

PANTRY PURGE

What's lurking behind closed doors? Often it's spoiled pantry staples, well past their expiration dates. Follow this guide to the shelf lives of opened products and learn when to toss that Tabasco.

Brown sugar: Indefinite.
Chocolate: 1 year.
Coffee (canned ground): 1 month.
Coffee beans: 3 weeks.
Honey: Indefinite.
Ketchup: 6 months.
Maple syrup: 1 year.
Marshmallows: 3 months.
Mustard: 2 years.
Olive oil: 1 year.
Pasta (dried): 1 year.
Peanut butter: 3 months.
Peanuts: 2 weeks.
Protein bars: 1 year.
Tabasco: 5 years.
Tea bags: 2 years.
Soy sauce: 3 months.
Steak sauce: 1 year.
Vinegar: 3 1/2 years.
White rice: 2 years.
Worcestershire sauce: 2 years.

Cleaning Kitchen Accessories

With these kitchen staples, it's tempting to cheat. (A crumby toaster? Hide it in the cupboard.) Here's how to keep everyday appliances looking like new.

Blender, Mixer, and Food Processor

- Pop off the blades and any other removable parts and soak them in a sink filled with warm water and dishwashing liquid.
- Hand wash the blender carafe and the food-processor bowl in warm, soapy water. You can also wash them on the top rack of the dishwasher.
- Using a nylon brush, scour off particles caked onto the blades.
- Dry the pieces thoroughly with a clean towel or cloth to prevent rust.
- Wipe down the bases with a cloth dampened with water and dishwashing liquid. Never submerge them in water, since the machinery of the appliances could get damaged.

Coffeemaker

- Remove and wash the filter and the carafe with warm, soapy water, then replace them.
- To descale water deposits, pour two to three cups of water and an equal amount of white vinegar into the water chamber and hit the brew button.
- Turn the machine off halfway through the cycle and let the solution sit inside the chamber for an hour. Then turn it back on and complete the cycle.
- Run two cycles of plain water through the machine to rinse out any leftover vinegar before using it again for your morning brew.
- Wipe the outside with a cloth wet with water and dishwashing liquid.
- Dry with a clean cloth.

Dishwasher

- Pull out the racks and wipe down the interior with a cloth and warm, soapy water. Scrub the racks' wheels (where bacteria hide) with a toothbrush.
- Fill the detergent cup with white vinegar and run an empty cycle to wipe out lime deposits. You can also dump a packet of powdered lemonade into the detergent cup and run the washer empty. The citric acid breaks up stains.
- Dust the fan slats with a vacuum's brush attachment.
- If the door is plastic, wipe it with a cloth and all-purpose cleaner. For stainless steel, dampen a cloth with water and dishwashing liquid, wring it out, and wipe the door with the grain.
- Dry with a clean cloth.

Electric Can Opener

- Unplug, remove the cutting wheel and the lid cover, and soak them in warm water and dishwashing liquid in the sink.
- Loosen grit stuck on the pieces by scrubbing them with a nylon brush or a toothbrush. You can also use baking soda and water to scour the blade.
- Rinse the pieces with water.
- Dry the pieces thoroughly—especially the metal cutting wheel—with a clean cloth to avoid rust.
- Wipe down the base with a cloth dampened with dishwashing liquid and warm water. Never immerse the electrical base in water, which could short the fuse.

Microwave

- Place a coffee mug filled with water and a few slices of lemon in the center of the microwave and run the machine on high power for three minutes. Let the lemon water sit inside for three more minutes. The steam will soften food spills, and the lemon aroma will eliminate odors.
- Wipe down the walls with a cloth soaked in warm, soapy water.
- Remove the turntable and scrub the wheels with a toothbrush.
- Wipe the exterior of plastic machines with a cloth sprayed with all-purpose cleaner, making sure to clean the fan slats. For stainless-steel machines, dip a cloth in water and dishwashing liquid, wring it out, and wipe with the grain.
- Buff dry with a clean cloth.

Toaster and Toaster Oven

- Unplug the appliance and empty the crumb tray.
- Remove the toaster-oven racks and soak them in warm, soapy water, scrubbing off any charred food with a sponge or a brush.
- Wipe the oven interior with a cloth wet with water and dishwashing liquid. Dislodge burned-on food with a toothbrush or an old credit card. Reach into the slots of a regular toaster with a wet pastry brush.
- Remove the knobs and soak them in soapy water. Dry and replace them.
- Wipe the outside of either appliance with a soapy cloth, scrubbing around levers, knobs, and door hinges using a toothbrush. If the exterior is chrome, crumple a ball of aluminum foil (shiny side out) and rub off rust spots.

Bathroom

Bathroom humor is lost on you—and for good reason. Cleaning the toilet can seem like a cruel joke. So much so that you're tempted to plunk one of those leave-in fresheners into the tank to do the work for you. But don't believe the hype. Not only can tablets damage the flush valve on your toilet, but they can also produce a gummy residue if left in for too long. So in the end, for all your pipe dreams, you'll be forced to scrub even more scum. The only way to really keep things spick-and-span—sorry to report—is to scour that tub, sink, and, yes, toilet with as much strength as you can muster. Let the poor, uninformed soul next door muscle the goop from her toilet. Who's laughing now?■

Bathroom Cleaning 101

When you look through the looking glass, do you like what you see? Once the mirror (and the tub and the sink and the floor) sparkle, you certainly will.

Step 1: Spray the tub and the shower with cleaner, and scrub the walls and the basin in a circular motion from top to bottom. (See Cleaning Your Tub, page 53, and Cleaning Your Shower, page 51, for cleaners and methods.) Spray the entire area with plain water to rinse off the cleaner, and wipe it down again with a damp cloth.

Step 2: Shine the mirror with a cloth spritzed with glass cleaner or dipped in dishwashing liquid and water. (See Cleaning Bathroom Accessories, page 54, for methods.)

Step 3: Wipe the sink and the vanity top with a damp cloth and dishwashing liquid or cleaner. (See Cleaning Your Sink and Vanity Top, page 47, for cleaners.) Rinse the cloth thoroughly and go over the area a second time. Scrub the drain with a toothbrush, and scrape buildup from the joints between the sink and the counter with the edge of an old credit card. Drains and overflow holes can collect grime, so circle them with a cotton swab moistened with dishwashing liquid.

Step 4: Disinfect and scrub both the inside and the outside of the toilet. (See Cleaning Bathroom Accessories, page 54, for methods.) Or, to save time, try this super bowl idea: Toss two antacid tablets into the toilet, let them dissolve for 20 minutes, then brush stains away with a toilet brush. Just as they do in your stomach, the antacids will dissolve the acids present, releasing them from the bowl.

Step 5: Mop the floor with a sponge mop and cleaner diluted in water, starting from the farthest corner of the room, working toward the door, and going from left to right. (See Floors, page 93, for cleaners.) Dip the mop into the bucket of cleaner, wring it out, and push it over a manageable section of the floor. Then dip the mop into a pail of clean water, wring it out, and mop the section again.

Step 6: Spray both the inside and the outside of the wastebasket with all-purpose cleaner, and wipe it down with a cloth.

THE 10-MINUTE CLEAN

While your family camps out in front of the TV, hog the bathroom during commercial breaks. Here's what you can do in only three sets of ads.

- Wipe out the sink.
- Wipe the mirror and the faucet.
- Swab a toilet brush around the bowl.
- Wipe the toilet seat and the outer rim.
- Spray the shower with cleaner and run a dry squeegee down the walls.

Bathroom Cleaning: Next Steps

With a little added legwork (and some magic faucet-shining techniques), your bathroom will gleam as you bubble over with excitement.

Step 1: Wipe down the shower rod, whether it is plastic or metal, with a cloth dampened with water and dishwashing liquid. Dust can build up, then stick to shower-curtain rings, preventing them from gliding smoothly over the rod.

Step 2: Empty the medicine cabinet and place the contents in the sink. Mist the walls and the shelves with cleaner and wipe them with a cloth. Scrub any dirty areas with a toothbrush. (See Cleaning Bathroom Accessories, page 54, for methods.)

Step 3: Clean the cabinets, if you have any, with a cloth lightly dampened with water and cleaner, going in the direction of the grain from top to bottom. (See Cleaning Your Cabinets and Drawers, page 37, for the right cleaners.) Rinse out the cloth, wring it out, and repeat. Polish the knobs.

Step 4: Fix up the faucet and the fixtures by wiping them with a cloth spritzed with cleaner. (See Cleaning Your Faucet and Fixtures, page 49, for the appropriate cleaners.) Buff with a clean cloth.

Step 5: Unclog the air vents by dusting or vacuuming them with a brush attachment. The more steam that can be sucked up by the vents means the less mold and mildew that will grow.

And for Extra Credit

EVERY MONTH

- Wipe down the moldings. (For methods, see page 85.)
- Disinfect the switch plates and wipe the doorknobs with a cloth and dishwashing liquid. (See page 85.)
- Dust the door frames and jambs.

EVERY SIX MONTHS

- Launder the shower curtain in the washing machine.
- Sweep the ceiling with an extendable duster. (For techniques, see page 83.)

Cleaning Your Sink and Vanity Top

Vanity isn't the most attractive trait. But conceit about your shiny sink? Certainly that won't be held against you. Find your finish and follow the steps.

Antique Porcelain and Porcelain Enamel

- Spritz a microfiber cloth with all-purpose cleaner and wipe the sink from the top to the drain in a circular motion. Don't use abrasive pads, cleansers, or wire brushes, all of which can scratch the finish. Scrub the drain with a toothbrush.
- Spray the surface with water and dry with a clean cloth.

Ceramic and Stone (Granite, Limestone, and Marble)

- Soak a cloth with water, wring it out, and apply dishwashing liquid. Starting at the top and working to the drain, rub in a circular motion. On stone, avoid using abrasive cleansers, which can scratch the surface; ammonia or nonchlorine bleach, which can dull it; and vinegar- and lemon-based cleaners, which can eat through it. Circle the drain with a toothbrush.
- Spray the entire surface with water and wipe with a clean cloth.

Fireclay and Vitreous China

- Spritz glass cleaner on a cloth and wipe the sink in a circular motion from the top to the drain. Scrub the drain with a toothbrush.
- Spray the entire surface with water and dry with a clean cloth.

Solid Surfaces (Such as Avonite and Corian)

HIGH-GLOSS FINISH

- Dip a cloth in a mixture of one part white vinegar and one part water and wring it out. Wipe the sink from top to bottom in a circular motion.

MATTE AND SATIN FINISHES

- Dampen a cloth with water and a few drops of dishwashing liquid, wring it out, and wipe the sink using the technique for a high-gloss finish. Avoid products with bleach, which can leave spots.
- Spray the entire surface with water and wipe with a clean cloth.

(To find out how to remove stains from these surfaces, see Stains, page 100.)

WHISTLE WHILE YOU WORK

Studies have shown that listening to music while working can improve your performance and help you complete tasks more quickly. Best of all, it puts you in a better mood. Before you scrub the sink, download these appropriate tunes.

"Another One Bites the Dust," Queen

"Clean," Depeche Mode

"Come Clean," Hilary Duff

"Drops From the Faucet," Nanci Griffith

"In the Bath," Edie Brickell

"Into the Groove," Madonna

"Scrub a Dub," Eric Hansen

"Shine On," Ryan Cabrera

"Suds in the Bucket," Sara Evans

"Talk Dirty to Me," Poison

"The Dirty Boogie," the Brian Setzer Orchestra

"Tiny Bubbles," Don Ho

"Wash, Mama, Wash," Dr. John

"Wipe Out," Surfaris

Cleaning Your Faucet and Fixtures

When itsy-bitsy mineral deposits climb up the waterspout, it doesn't take much to wash them out. (Just don't use ammonia or abrasive cleansers.)

Brass

- Apply dishwashing liquid to a damp cloth and wipe down the faucet.
- Use a cotton swab to clean the edges and the mounting. Dental floss can break up hardened deposits in crevices.
- If the fixture is unlacquered, polish it by smoothing brass cream onto a cloth and rubbing the fixture. (Dab a bit of polish onto an inconspicuous spot with a white cloth. If the cloth turns black, the faucet is unlacquered.)
- Wipe with a damp cloth and dry with a clean cloth.

Bronze and Gold Plated

- Follow the technique for brass, but omit the brass cream.

Chrome

- Spray with clean water and wipe down the faucet with a cloth, using a cotton swab or dental floss to clean the edges and the mounting.
- For extra shine, spray glass cleaner onto a cloth and wipe the faucet.

Copper

- Apply dishwashing liquid to a damp cloth and wipe down the faucet, using cotton swabs or dental floss to clean the edges and the mounting.
- Apply a commercial copper polish (available at hardware stores) to a soft cloth and rub the faucet, following the package instructions.

Nickel

- Rub a clean, dry cloth over water and mineral deposits to buff them out.
- Use a cotton swab or dental floss to clean the edges and the mounting.
- Spray glass cleaner onto a cloth, wipe the fixture, and allow it to air-dry.

Stainless Steel

- Wet a cloth with warm water and a few drops of dishwashing liquid, and rub the fixture to lift dirt.
- Blot dry with a clean cloth to prevent water deposits from forming.
- Apply a thin layer of stainless-steel polish, following the package instructions, and wipe off any excess immediately.
- Buff the polish onto the faucet with a clean, dry cloth.

KETCHUP CAN SHINE FAUCETS
No kidding. Here, seven more surprising household helpers that add luster to your hardware.
Baby oil: Oil a cloth and rub on chrome.
Flour, salt, and vinegar: How to polish brass, bronze, and copper? Mix one tablespoon each of flour, salt, and vinegar. Smear the paste onto a damp cloth and wipe. Spray with water and buff.
Ketchup: Squirt a bit on a cloth and rub on copper. Rinse with a damp cloth. The acetic acid in ketchup dissolves the oxide tarnish that makes copper look cloudy.
Lemon: Cut a lemon in half, sprinkle it with a dash of salt, and rub it on brass and copper. Buff with a clean cloth.
Toothpaste: Squeeze plain white paste onto a damp cloth and rub on chrome. Buff dry.
WD-40: Apply the lubricant to a cloth and wipe on stainless steel.
White vinegar: Pour a bit onto a cloth and rub on chrome faucets. The acid dissolves soap scum.

Cleaning Your Shower

No wonder the most frightening scene in the movie *Psycho* happened in the shower—it can be a scary place. Make sure yours has a happy ending.

Doors

FIBERGLASS AND GLASS

- Remove soap scum by dipping a scrub brush in white vinegar and rubbing the surface in circles from top to bottom.
- Pour lemon oil onto a cloth and wipe the door in circles to erase lime scale.
- Spray glass cleaner onto the door and wipe it with a cloth.

LAMINATED GLASS AND TEMPERED GLASS

- Follow the technique above, starting with the lemon oil. Vinegar can burn laminated glass, which consists of a plastic sheet between two pieces of glass.

Door Runners and Tracks

- Saturate a low-grade steel-wool pad or a toothbrush with dishwashing liquid and scrub inside and outside the door runners from left to right.
- Go over the area again with a wet cloth, then dry with a clean one.

Showerhead

- Unscrew the nozzle. Pour vinegar in a plastic grocery bag and immerse the head. Tie the handles in a knot over the shaft and secure with rubber bands.
- Soak the head overnight to dissolve lime stains.
- In the morning, scrub off slime and rust with a toothbrush and water. Poke out hardened mineral deposits stuck in the perforations with a toothpick.
- Rinse thoroughly with water in the sink and reconnect the showerhead.

Tile

GLAZED CERAMIC

- Spray black mildew spots with tile cleaner with bleach. Let it work for five minutes. When it dries, the mildew should be gone—without scrubbing.
- Wipe down the area with a cloth saturated with water to rinse the bleach.
- Mix one capful of rubbing alcohol with one gallon of water, and dunk a scrub brush into the solution. Work over the entire span of tile in circular strokes, scrubbing hardest around the drain. Oil soaps and ammonia can yellow grout, and vinegar can damage it, so avoid all of them.

UNGLAZED

- Follow the steps above, with one exception: Instead of using rubbing alcohol and water, dilute a squirt of dishwashing liquid in a gallon of water.

DOUBLE-DUTY SHOWER PRODUCTS Singing the blues in the shower because your products are spilling over the caddy? Consolidate with these multitaskers. **Bath salts as a body scrub:** Finely ground salts (try sea salt or even Epsom salts) won't irritate skin when used with a loofah. **Hair conditioner as a shave gel:** Razors glide with ease over the gooey formula, and the vitamins and nutrients that nourish your scalp will do the same for your legs. **Baby shampoo as eye-makeup remover:** No more tears. The incredibly gentle gel removes waterproof mascaras without irritating eyes.

Cleaning Your Tub

Who cares about the butcher, the baker, and the candlestick maker? Here's how to get all *your* (rubber) ducks in a row, whatever your type of tub.

Acrylic and Fiberglass

- Make a paste of cream of tartar and a 3 percent hydrogen peroxide solution (the concentration sold in drugstores). Dip a cloth in the paste and scrub rust stains.
- Squirt a mildly abrasive creamy cleanser directly onto the tub. Let it sit for five minutes to penetrate the surface. Never use vinegar, as it can dissolve the nonskid surface of the tub.
- Working from top to bottom and back to front, spread the cleanser onto the sides of the tub by making circles with a cloth.
- Mimic the technique on the floor of the tub, scrubbing the area around the drain as much as possible, since dirt pools there. If necessary, use a toothbrush to remove grime.
- Douse the tub with clean water using a handheld showerhead or a spray bottle, making sure to rinse off the cleanser completely.
- Dry the surface with a clean cloth or a towel to prevent mineral deposits and lime-scale buildup.

Enameled Steel, Porcelain Enamel, and Stone (Granite, Limestone, and Marble)

- Drench a cloth with warm water and a small amount of dishwashing liquid. Starting at the top back of the tub and working to the drain, rub the surface in a circular motion and apply pressure as needed. Scrub the area around the drain using a toothbrush. Don't use abrasive pads, cleansers, or wire brushes, which can scratch the finish. Avoid vinegar- and lemon-based cleansers and bleach, which can eat through stone.
- Dry with a clean cloth to prevent mineral deposits and lime-scale growth.

Slate

- Pour $\frac{1}{2}$ cup of ammonia into one gallon of warm water. Saturate a cloth with the mixture and rub the tub from the top to the drain in circles to eradicate soap scum. Never use abrasive cleansers, vinegar- or lemon-based cleansers, or vinegar itself, all of which could damage the finish.
- Dunk a cloth in water and squirt dishwashing liquid onto the cloth. Rub the tub from the top to the drain in circles. Scrub the drain with a toothbrush.
- Dry thoroughly with a clean cloth.

KILLING MILDEW

Try as you might, those black mildew stains won't come clean. That's probably because they have grown between the caulk and the tile. Your only choice? Remove the caulk. Here's how.

- Scrape away the caulk with a caulk-remover tool (sold at hardware stores).
- Soak a cloth in rubbing alcohol and run it along the tile to kill mildew. Wipe with a damp cloth and let dry overnight.
- Put on rain boots, fill the tub with water, and stand in it. (This weighs down the tub, exposing the most space between the tub and tile, so you can caulk completely.)
- Line painter's tape on the top and bottom of the empty caulk space.
- Squeeze the caulk into the entire groove.
- Squirt a little bit of dishwashing liquid in a bowl of water and wet your fingertips. Smooth out the caulk with your fingertips, then slowly pull away the tape.
- Leave the tub full of water for 24 hours and let the caulk dry.

Cleaning Bathroom Accessories

Caution: Objects in the mirror may be dirtier than they appear. Keep the grime at a safe distance by sticking to these routines.

Fixtures

- Wet a cloth with water, squirt dishwashing liquid onto it, and wipe the towel racks, toilet-paper holder, hooks, and other fixtures.
- Work around wall mountings with a wet toothbrush, if necessary.
- Dry with a clean cloth to prevent mineral deposits.

Medicine Cabinet

- Wipe the walls and the shelves (tops and undersides) of the empty cabinet with a cloth spritzed with all-purpose cleaner.
- Dry with a clean cloth.
- If the door is wood, wipe it with a damp cloth and dishwashing liquid, applying pressure to any toothpaste splatters. If it is glass, spray glass cleaner onto a cloth and wipe it in a circular motion. For a mirrored door, see Mirror, below.

Mirror

- Mix one part white vinegar and one part warm water in a bucket and dip a cloth in the solution. Or spray glass cleaner onto a cloth or a crumpled piece of newspaper. Refrain from spraying cleaner directly onto the mirror, because excess liquid can seep behind the edges, causing black spots to appear on the reflective surface.
- Wipe the mirror in a circular motion, working from the outside of the mirror in and from top to bottom.
- If residue from toothpaste or hair spray persists, rub those spots with a cloth wet with hot water. The water should be enough to buff them out.
- Dry thoroughly with a clean cloth or a coffee filter to prevent streaks.

Plastic Shower-Curtain Liner

▪ Take down the liner and place it in the washing machine with old towels. The towels will agitate the liner, scrubbing off soap scum.

▪ Run the washing machine on a hot-water soaking cycle and pour in ¾ cup of bleach when water fills the machine. Detergent isn't necessary; the bleach should kill mold and mildew and remove stains.

▪ If any mildew remains after machine washing, make a paste of baking soda and water, smear it onto a cloth, and rub it on the growth.

▪ Wipe the liner with a wet cloth to rinse off the baking-soda solution.

Sink Accessories

▪ Most containers, whether plastic, porcelain, or stainless steel, can be cleaned with a cloth dampened with dishwashing liquid and water.

▪ Get into the grooves of toothbrush holders and the edges of soap dishes with a cotton swab or a pipe cleaner.

▪ Dry the pieces with a clean cloth to prevent mineral deposits.

Toilet

▪ Pour a bucket of water in the toilet to flush out the water.

▪ Gently rub a natural pumice stone (available at hardware stores) on rust and hard-water stains in the bowl. To avoid scratching, keep the stone moist.

▪ Squirt toilet-bowl cleaner or a mildly abrasive creamy cleanser around the inner rim and swab the bowl, rim, and drain with a toilet brush.

▪ Flush the toilet. The cleaner can corrode the bowl's glaze if it sits too long.

▪ Spray all-purpose cleaner onto a cloth and wipe the commode, scrubbing the screw coverings at the bottom with a toothbrush.

▪ Wipe the seat with the same cloth, and scrub around the hinges with a toothbrush. Rinse the area with a wet cloth and buff dry.

Living Room, Dining Room, and Bedrooms

Some surprising finds are unexpected moments of good fortune: the $20 bill stashed in a coat pocket since last winter, for example, or an extra quarter's worth of minutes left on a vacant parking meter. Others, like a moldy clump of raisins beneath a sofa cushion or a half-inch layer of dust on top of the ceiling-fan blades, are not as delightful. As the main hub of activity in your home, your living and dining rooms and bedrooms show signs of their use. And the extras that make the rooms beautiful—chandeliers, fireplace, electronics—lose their luster over time. But if you set aside a few minutes here and there to clean these rooms, you can avoid at least one unwanted surprise: dirt sneaking up on you. ∎

Living-Room, Dining-Room, and Bedroom Cleaning 101

You can burn off an entire Sunday brunch by tackling these tasks. (Who needs to watch four hours of football, anyway?)

Step 1: Clear the dust off the furnishings. Start with the furniture (tables, dressers, bookshelves) and move on to the electronics (stereo, television, cable box), wiping down the outsides with a microfiber cloth. Don't worry too much about the insides; you'll get to them another day. (See Cleaning Your Furniture, page 63, and Cleaning Living-Area Accessories, page 70, for cleaners and methods.)

Step 2: Squeeze excess liquid from a disinfecting wipe into the sink; use the wipe to sterilize the telephone. The receiver traps germs in the perforated ear- and mouthpieces. Swipe the cloth over remote controls for electronics and video-game equipment. It's easy to overlook clickers, but the keys are hot buttons for dirt and bacteria, since they come in contact with hands. (See Cleaning Living-Area Accessories, page 70, for details.)

Step 3: Wipe down upholstered pieces, including your sofa, dining-room chairs, and ottomans, with a moistened microfiber cloth. If they seem unusually soiled, go over the fabric with a dry-cleaning sponge. (See Cleaning Your Upholstery, page 65, for cleaners and methods.)

Step 4: Wash the windows with glass cleaner spritzed on newspaper or use a solution of dishwashing liquid and water and a squeegee. (See Windows, page 87, for techniques.)

Step 5: Change the bedsheets or shake them out over the bedroom floor, which will kick out unwelcome bedmates—dust and dust mites. Then vacuum the floor in the bedroom, especially around the perimeter of the bed, which is a haven for dust mites. (See Floors, page 93, for vacuuming techniques specific to carpet and other types of flooring.) Maneuver the vacuum through the entire living space, using a brush attachment on uncarpeted areas. You can also dust-mop hardwood floors if you wish.

THE 10-MINUTE CLEAN
While dinner is in the oven and the six-o'clock news blares in the background, you can quickly complete these chores.
- Dust the tabletops and spot-clean the cabinet fronts whenever you see fingerprints.
- Dust all surfaces, electronics, books, blinds, and picture frames.
- Vacuum the rugs and the carpets or dust-mop the floors.

PEST CONTROL
Here's how to give ants (and other common pests) marching orders.
Ants: Colonies of the most common pest come in search of sustenance. Check sink pipes for leaks. Loose gaskets are the top entry point for ants. Leave out one cup of honey mixed with one teaspoon of boric acid and the ants will be history in no time.
Mice: Seeking warmth and food, mice can wriggle in through nickel-size holes in air-conditioning and water lines, so seal them shut. When mice get inside, set glue traps or humane live traps (sold at hardware stores).
Roaches: After hitching a ride on paper bags and provisions from the grocery store, the nocturnal nuisances track germs—up to 33 types—into your home. Seal trash in cans and patch cracks in moldings. If they do get in, call an exterminator. (For tips on dealing with other insects, turn to What's *Really* on Your Counter?, page 25.)

Living-Room, Dining-Room, and Bedroom Cleaning: Next Steps

When the kids are on playdates and you've got the house to yourself, fit in these advanced steps before settling down with that fat novel.

Step 1: Swipe an extendable duster over light fixtures, ceiling fans, and recessed lighting. Be sure to turn them off before you dust. (See Cleaning Your Fans and Lights, page 67, for methods.) You may want to shield your eyes from billowing dust by wearing glasses or goggles.

Step 2: Vacuum drapes and blinds on a low setting with a brush attachment. (See Window Coverings, page 89.) A quicker (though less effective) method is to wipe them with an extendable duster or a dry-cleaning sponge.

Step 3: Open furniture doors and drawers and dust the insides with a cloth and cleaner. (See Cleaning Your Furniture, page 63, for cleaners.)

Step 4: Dust artwork frames with a duster or a dust-mop cloth. Spritz glass cleaner onto a microfiber cloth or a wad of newspaper and wipe the glass. (See Cleaning Living-Area Accessories, page 70, for techniques.) Use a blow-dryer on the cool setting to blow dust off sculptures.

Step 5: Vacuum mattresses and box springs using the brush attachment. Go over the entire surface in long, horizontal strokes, paying special attention to the indented or buttoned areas, where dust and dust mites get stuck.

Step 6: Vacuum the areas usually out of eyesight. Lift big pieces of furniture and vacuum underneath. Appliance wheels or casters come in handy for moving heavy sofas and chairs. (See Floors, page 93, for methods.)

And for Extra Credit

EVERY MONTH
- Dust the moldings. (See page 85 for methods.)
- Dust the door frames and jambs.
- Vacuum the heating and air-conditioning vents.
- Wipe down the switch plates and the doorknobs with a soapy cloth.

EVERY SIX MONTHS
- Sweep the ceilings. (For techniques, see page 83.)

Cleaning Your Furniture

Should the dust settle on your precious pieces of furniture, follow this advice to get all kinds of finishes back in tip-top shape.

Acrylic

▪ Dampen a cloth with water and a squirt of dishwashing liquid. Wring it out well and wipe the piece of furniture from top to bottom. Avoid solvents, ammonia, and vinegar, all of which can dissolve the coating or the finish.

Antique Wood

▪ Wet a cloth with distilled water and wring it out well, as excess water can warp wood. Wipe the piece in long strokes from top to bottom.
▪ Buff with a clean cloth.

Hard Finishes (Lacquer, Polyurethane) and Painted Wood

▪ Dust the furniture from top to bottom with a microfiber cloth.
▪ Mix one teaspoon of dishwashing liquid with one gallon of water, dampen a cloth with the solution, then wring it out. Wipe the piece of furniture from top to bottom to remove any ingrained dirt.

Oil Finishes

▪ Dust the entire piece from top to bottom with a microfiber cloth.
▪ Douse a cloth with odorless mineral spirits (a solvent, sold at hardware stores, that thins oil finishes and removes grime). Wipe from top to bottom.

Shellac and Varnish Finishes

▪ Dust the piece from top to bottom with a microfiber cloth.
▪ Dampen a cloth with mineral spirits and rub the surface in circular strokes, from top to bottom. Or use a cloth that has been dipped in a solution of one teaspoon of dishwashing liquid and one gallon of water, then wrung out well.

Wicker

▪ Vacuum the surface from top to bottom with a brush attachment.
▪ Mix two tablespoons of dishwashing liquid in a bucket of cool water. Dip in a cloth and wring it out very well. Wipe the piece from top to bottom.
▪ For deeper cleaning, call a professional.

(To find out how to remove stains from furniture, see Stains, page 105.)

TO WAX OR NOT TO WAX?

That is the question. Look at the finish of your furniture for the answer. **Oil finishes:** Apply a high-quality paste wax (sold at hardware stores) every two to four years. For parts that are used heavily, like tabletops, apply once a year. Paste wax provides a long-lasting finish that repels water and dust. Ball up a cloth and smear on the wax. Rub a thin layer on the surface. When it's dry, buff with a cloth. **Shellac and varnish finishes:** The mineral spirits you use to clean these pieces can dissolve the finish, so apply wax after cleaning. But first remove old wax with a dewaxer (a deep-cleaning solvent, sold at hardware stores), so the new coat goes on better. Then follow the steps above for applying paste wax. **Polyurethane finishes:** Fairly resistant to moisture, these pieces don't require waxing.

Cleaning Your Upholstery

All love seats, ottomans, and sofas are not cut from the same cloth. Some need lots of attention, while others don't like to be touched.

Canvas, Jacquard, and Rayon

- Run a dry-cleaning sponge over the fabric in short, even strokes to lift ingrained dirt. Be gentle on Jacquard, since delicate yarns can pull and snag.
- Add two capfuls of mild detergent to a bucket of cool water. Dip in a sponge or cloth, wring it out well, and go back and forth over the fabric with long strokes. Use as little liquid as possible, since wet fabric can sprout mildew.
- Let the pieces air-dry.

Leather and Vinyl

- Vacuum the piece of furniture on a low setting with a brush attachment.
- Rub soiled areas with a microfiber cloth that is slightly dampened with water. Water can remove dirt but won't permanently discolor the leather.
- For deeper cleaning, call a professional upholstery cleaner. (See Resources, page 117, to locate one in your area.)

Pile Fabrics (Chenille and Corduroy) and Wool

- Vacuum the piece on a low setting with an upholstery attachment in long, horizontal strokes from top to bottom. Do not use the vacuum's hard-bristle brush attachment, since it can pull on fabric.
- For deeper cleaning, consult a professional. (See Resources, page 117.)

Slipcovers

COTTON AND LINEN

- Remove the covers and machine wash them on a delicate setting, following the care instructions on the label, which is usually attached near the zipper.

SILK

- Hand wash the covers in a sink filled with warm water and a capful of delicate laundry detergent. Or have the covers dry-cleaned.

Suede

- Clean suede using a product recommended by the manufacturer. Avoid using any moisture on suede, since it will be permanently stained.
- For deeper cleaning, consult a professional. (See Resources, page 117.)

(To find out how to remove stains from upholstery, see Stains, page 103.)

FABRIC CLEANING CODES

Before testing any cleaner on fabric, consult the cheat sheet affixed to the piece of furniture to make sure it's safe. Though the tag isn't required by law, most manufacturers voluntarily attach one under seat cushions and near slipcover zippers. On it is a cleaning code devised by industry professionals. Find the upholstery code and follow these directions to the letter.

Code S: Never use water. Instead, spot-clean with a mild water-free solvent (available at home-improvement centers).

Code S-W: Use either a water-free solvent or a water-based cleaner or foam (available at home-improvement centers).

Code W: Water-based cleaners and distilled water can be used. (Tap water contains minerals that can cause fading.)

Code X: X marks the spot where cleaners should not go. Vacuum these fabrics carefully.

Cleaning Your Fans and Lights

Light travels at approximately 299 million meters per second. Luckily, you don't need a physics degree to complete these speedy steps in record time.

Ceiling Fans

- Angle the head of an extendable duster to dust the tops of the blades.
- Use a ladder to wipe blades with a cloth sprayed with all-purpose cleaner.
- Unscrew the ceiling mount of the light fixture, if your fan has one, and wash it in the sink with warm water and dishwashing liquid. Rinse it in cold water and dry it before reattaching. (Moisture can rust the screw sockets.)

Chandeliers

- Dust the hardware and the crystals with a dry, lint-free cloth.
- If the chandelier is extremely dirty, take it apart and individually soak each crystal in rubbing alcohol for 30 minutes to one hour. If the crystals can't be removed, dip a cloth in rubbing alcohol and wipe them down.
- Slip on lint-free gloves and individually dry each crystal with a microfiber cloth. (You'll be grateful for the gloves—no fingerprints.) Rehang the crystals.

Dome Lights and Pendants

- Dust the hardware and the wall-hanging cord with an extendable duster.
- Spritz a cloth with ammonia-free glass cleaner and wipe the dome gently.

Fluorescent and Track Lighting

- Dust the hardware and the bulbs with an extendable duster.
- Unscrew the metal ceiling mounts and wipe them with a cloth wet with water and dishwashing liquid. Reattach them.

Lamps

BASE

- No matter the material, wipe the base with a cloth dampened with water.

SHADE

- Vacuum shades on a low setting with a brush attachment in long, vertical strokes. Or use a dry-cleaning sponge.
- To clean a fabric shade, roll it from side to side in a tub filled with a few inches of lukewarm water and two capfuls of delicate laundry detergent. Distribute the liquid evenly over the shade with a cloth. Rinse with a damp cloth.
- Gently blot the inside and the outside with a white or colorfast towel.
- Lay the towel on the floor and set the shade on it right-side up to dry.

LIGHTING SAFETY TIPS

While doing a little light housekeeping, abide by these safety tips. That way, the only shock you'll get will be seeing how brightly the lights shine.

- Always unplug lamps before cleaning any part. Touching plugged-in appliances with wet hands puts you at risk of electrical shock. Frayed cords can also give you a jolt.
- When cleaning wall-mounted lights, turn off the electricity at the fuse box. It's the only way to stop current from surging through the fixture.
- Before cleaning lamps and wall-mounted fixtures, cover sockets with plastic bags secured with rubber bands. Water can short the fuse. If a socket gets soggy, do not turn on the electricity. Ask an electrician to assess its safety before using it.
- In your bathrooms and kitchen, consider installing ground-fault circuit interrupters, which safeguard against shock. The devices (sold at hardware stores) cost less than $30 each.

Cleaning Your Fireplace

Where there's a fireplace, there's smoke. Soot and ash, too. Read on for answers to your burning questions about how to clean the hearth.

Electric and Gas Fireplaces

INTERIOR

- Contact your local hearth-products dealer each year for a tune-up, since carbon buildup is flammable. (See Resources, page 117, to find a technician.)

EXTERIOR

- Wipe the outside with a cloth wet with water and dishwashing liquid.
- Buff the glass door, if you have one, with a cloth to prevent streaking.

Pellet-Burning Stove

INTERIOR

- Empty the ash drawer and the ash trap (located on the back), following the instructions in the care manual. (Different brands require different tactics.)
- Have the stove, motors, fans, and vents cleaned each year by a professional, since the parts can easily be broken. (See Resources, page 117, to find a pro.)

EXTERIOR

- Follow the technique for cleaning the exterior of an electric or gas fireplace.

Wood-Burning Fireplace and Stove

INTERIOR

- Shovel or sweep out ashes with a metal dustpan or a hearth shovel and place them in a metal bucket or ash bin. Dump them in the garden as fertilizer or have the local hazardous–household-waste system pick them up. (See Resources, page 117, for more information.)
- Sweep the hearth with a broom, brushing ashes and dust into a dustpan.
- Brush off creosote—the black powder clinging to the walls of the firebox, which is a highly flammable wood emission—with a stiff-bristle plastic brush. Do not use any cleaners, which could cause fumes and combustion.
- Once a year, have the chimney swept. (See Resources, page 117.)

EXTERIOR

- Vacuum a metal or wrought-iron screen with a brush attachment. Wipe a glass screen from top to bottom with a cloth spritzed with glass cleaner.
- Clean the shell of a wood-burning stove with a cream cleaner (available at hearth dealers), following the instructions on the label.
- Wipe glass doors and the mantel with a cloth wet with water and dish soap.
- Buff the doors with a clean cloth to prevent streaking.

STOP SMOKE SMELLS

When the stench lingers long after the flames have died, try these two tricks to snuff it.

If your chimney smells: A bottle of chimney deodorant (usually $10 or less at hearth-supply or hardware stores) is topped with a chemical-emitting wick that absorbs the creosote scent for two to three months. Set the bottle in the fireplace when it's not in use. An aerosol smoke eliminator (also available at hardware stores) can neutralize smoky smells in a fireplace. Just spray it up the damper.

If your curtains, drapes, and upholstery smell: Some dry cleaners are equipped with spaces called ozone rooms, in which they can perform a special deodorizing process. The complicated (but not terribly expensive) process produces an oxidizing agent that creates a pleasant scent to neutralize smoke odors on fabric.

Cleaning Living-Area Accessories

For the ensemble of things that entertain you, a little effort goes a long way toward keeping them operating at peak performance.

Artwork and Frames

- Dust paintings and sculptures with a clean, dry piece of muslin (available at craft stores). Muslin is incredibly gentle and isn't treated with chemicals or fabric softeners, so it won't damage artwork. You can also blow off dust with a blow-dryer on a cool setting held a few inches away from the artwork.
- If a painting is protected by glass, spritz a cloth with mild, ammonia-free glass cleaner and wipe in horizontal strokes from top to bottom. Never spray glass cleaner directly onto the glass, as it could drip, leak into crevices, and dissolve the paint.
- Gently dust frames with a duster or a soft cloth dampened with water.

DVD Player and VCR

- Dust the outsides of electronics with a soft electrostatic dust-mop cloth lightly moistened with dishwashing liquid and water, making sure to wipe all buttons and knobs. Do not use any abrasives or solvents, such as rubbing alcohol, since they can damage the metal finish.
- Insert a videotape-head cleaner or a DVD-lens cleaner and press Play.
- Spray the vents of the machines with a can of compressed air (available at office-supply stores) to remove dust, holding the canister a few inches away from the machine at about a 45-degree angle.
- Open the tray or the cartridge door and spray with a can of compressed air at about a 45-degree angle to remove dust.

iPod Dock

- Unplug the dock and wipe it down with a damp soft, lint-free cloth. Liquids should not be used on iPod docks, since they can seep through the cracks and damage the machinery. Aerosol sprays, solvents, and abrasives can mar the finish.

Remote Controls

- Squeeze excess liquid from a disinfecting wipe into the sink. Wipe the entire surface of the remote control, including the front, the back, the sides, and the buttons.
- Dip a cotton swab in rubbing alcohol, pinch off the excess moisture with your finger, and circle the sides and the tops of the buttons to dissolve sticky patches and grime.

Stereo and Speakers

- Dust the entire surface of the stereo, including the knobs, by wiping everything with an electrostatic dust-mop cloth that has been slightly dampened with water and a few drops of dishwashing liquid, then wrung out.
- Open the CD tray and spray the inside with a can of compressed air (available at electronic and office-supply stores) at about a 45-degree angle. This angle blows out the greatest amount of dust.
- Run a clean medium-size paintbrush with soft, natural bristles over the speakers from left to right to lift dust. You can also spray the speakers with a can of compressed air, using the above technique, but the paintbrush method often frees more dust and is just as safe.

Television

- Dust the screens of plasma, LCD, and standard television sets in long, horizontal strokes, beginning at the top of the screen, with a dry electrostatic dust-mop cloth or a dry-cleaning sponge. (Shorter strokes cause smudging.)
- Wipe the casing of the set with an electrostatic dust-mop cloth lightly spritzed with glass cleaner.
- To remove stubborn dirt, purchase a specialty screen wipe at an appliance or office-supply store and follow the package instructions.

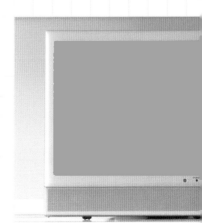

Laundry Room

At times, your laundry room is a bit like you. It does a lot of dirty work and rarely receives any glory. In go tablecloths caked with ketchup, workout clothes soaked with sweat, and the occasional pair of smelly sneakers. Out come loads of clean laundry as sweet smelling as a field of summertime honeysuckle. But the exhausted workhorse? It's often rusting around the machine edges, full of lint, and sprinkled with whatever crusty material came out of those jeans before they were tossed into the washer. Your laundry room doesn't take a break from its duties very often, so keep it running smoothly by paying attention to its many important parts. Not bad advice for you, too. ∎

Laundry-Room Cleaning 101

Doing the laundry may be a thankless task (just ask Cinderella), but spiffing up the room that churns out fresh linens can be rewarding. Really.

Step 1: Run white vinegar through the washer to sanitize the inside and clear away soap scum. (See Cleaning Laundry-Room Accessories, page 78, for specifics.) Just think: The average household washer and dryer launder about 400 full-size loads a year. That's a lot of gunk on the washer walls.

Step 2: Empty the dryer's lint trap by wiping off fuzz with a damp cloth or a used fabric-softener sheet. Or wet your hands and run your fingers over the mesh screen to scoop up the lint. Fabric softener can cause a waxy buildup on the screen, so wash it out in a sink or vacuum it. (See Cleaning Laundry-Room Accessories, page 78.)

Step 3: Wipe the interior walls of the dryer with a cloth dampened with dishwashing liquid and warm water. Scrub any linty residue around the trap opening with a toothbrush, if necessary. (See Cleaning Laundry-Room Accessories, page 78.)

Step 4: Wipe down the outside of each appliance—front, sides, top, and back—with a cloth dampened with a few drops of dishwashing liquid or all-purpose cleaner. (See Cleaning Laundry-Room Accessories, page 78.)

Step 5: Wash out the sink, if you have one, with cleaner and a cloth. (See Cleaning Your Sink, page 27.) Shine the faucet with a microfiber cloth. (See Cleaning Your Faucets and Fixtures, page 29.)

Step 6: Clean the countertop surfaces, shelving, and bins with a cloth and cleaner. (See Cleaning Laundry-Room Accessories, page 78.) Wipe down the cabinet fronts with a cloth and cleaner. (See Cleaning Your Cabinets and Drawers, page 37.)

Step 7: Mop or vacuum the floor, starting from the farthest corner of the room and working toward the door, from left to right. (See Floors, page 93, for cleaners and method.) Launder rugs, if possible, or vacuum them. Run a dust mop underneath the washer and the dryer, if it fits. Airborne lint can get kicked underneath the appliances and create a fire hazard if it piles up.

THE 10-MINUTE CLEAN

In about the time it takes for a spin cycle to finish, look what you can accomplish.

- Clean the lint trap.
- Wipe down the exterior of the washing machine and the dryer.
- Sanitize the inside of the washing machine.
- Dust all surfaces and shelving.

Laundry-Room Cleaning: Next Steps

You've mastered getting stains out of clothing. With the right tools and a little time, you'll now be able to say the same for the laundry room.

Step 1: Clean mineral deposits and spray-starch buildup from the iron by wiping it down with a paste of baking soda and water applied to a cloth. Circle the holes on the soleplate with cotton swabs. (See Cleaning Laundry-Room Accessories, page 78.)

Step 2: Run an extendable duster around the inside of the dryer hose to clear away the lint that accumulates on the walls. Or vacuum with a crevice attachment. (See Cleaning Laundry-Room Accessories, page 78.)

Step 3: Wash the windows with a cloth spritzed with glass cleaner or dishwashing liquid and water. (See Windows, page 87.) Pass over the sill and the frame with the damp cloth. Vacuum curtains, if you have them, with a brush attachment. (See Window Coverings, page 89.)

Step 4: On a low setting, with a brush attachment, vacuum the backs of the washing machine and the dryer and the flooring underneath. To reach behind the units, use appliance wheels or casters (available at hardware stores) to move the machines. Be careful not to stretch the dryer hose. If the hose looks too short, disconnect it first.

Step 5: Vacuum the vents on a high setting with a brush attachment. Dust and lint, particularly in this room, can clog the vents, reducing airflow in the room. Wipe the vent's grates with a damp cloth.

And for Extra Credit

EVERY MONTH
- Dust the moldings and the baseboards. (See page 85 for methods.)
- Dust the door frames and jambs.
- Wipe down the switch plates and the doorknobs with a cloth and dishwashing liquid.

EVERY SIX MONTHS
- Sweep the ceiling. (See page 83 for techniques.)

Cleaning Laundry-Room Accessories

Your ancestors scrubbed their socks riverside on washboards. Show a little appreciation for the conveniences that make your life a whole lot easier.

Dryer

- Smudge petroleum jelly on a cloth, then rub it into the folds of the rubber ring around the door to remove sticky residue.
- Remove the lint trap and clean it (see Lint Trap, opposite).
- Cover the opening of the trap with an old towel so that moisture does not get inside. Wipe down the interior walls with a soft cloth dampened with dishwashing liquid and water.
- Wipe down the enamel exterior, the front and the back of the door, and the area around the lint-trap opening with a cloth dampened with water and a few drops of dishwashing liquid.

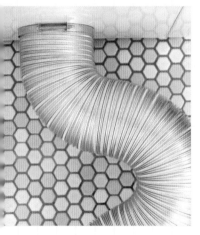

Dryer Hose

- Turn off the gas or electric supply, then pull the dryer away from the wall, being careful not to stretch the hose. Disconnect the hose from the back of the dryer by unscrewing the screws or the brackets. Hold the hose horizontally so that dust doesn't dump out the bottom.
- Shake out the lint into a wastebasket.
- Pass an extendable duster through the hose to collect any lint clinging to the inside walls. If the dust isn't too thick, vacuum it out with a crevice attachment. Do not skip this step; clogged hoses are a leading cause of dryer fires in homes.
- Reaffix the hose to the dryer.

Iron

- Check the manual for instructions, which vary by brand. Most, however, can tolerate this method: Make a paste of two tablespoons of baking soda and one tablespoon of water. Spread it on the soleplate. Wipe off with a damp cloth.
- Dip a cotton swab in distilled water and insert it into the steam holes.
- Fill the reservoir a third of the way with distilled water.
- Turn on the iron. Make sure nothing delicate is underneath the iron, as sediment from broken-down mineral deposits will drip out the bottom.
- Press the steam button until steam flows freely. Pour out leftover liquid.
- Steam an old, clean rag to make sure all the mineral deposits have been flushed out. Wipe the soleplate with a cloth and distilled water.

Lint Trap

- Take out the trap insert and remove the lint with a damp cloth or a used fabric-softener sheet. Or wet your hands and run your fingers over the mesh screen to scoop up the lint. Lint is highly combustible, so it is important to wipe the screen dry. Also, a clogged lint trap slows down the machine's drying time, causing it to use up to 30 percent more energy.
- Vacuum the mesh screen with a brush attachment on a low setting. Or wash it in the sink with water and dishwashing liquid.
- Dampen a cloth with water and dishwashing liquid and run it across the plastic edges of the trap. Scrub with a toothbrush if the edges are sticky.

Shelving

- Dust empty shelves with an extendable duster.
- On areas splattered with detergent or stain remover, rub with a cloth dampened with water and dishwashing liquid, applying pressure as needed.

Washing Machine

- Apply petroleum jelly on a cloth, then wipe it around the perimeter of the rubber ring to catch debris caught in the folds.
- Fill the washer with hot water (130 degrees Fahrenheit), add one gallon of white vinegar, and run a rinse cycle.
- Remove the knobs and the detergent dispenser, if possible, and wash them in warm water and dishwashing liquid in the sink. Or put them in the dishwasher. If the pieces are not removable, wipe them with a cloth spritzed with all-purpose cleaner.
- Wipe down the enamel exterior and the front and the back of the door with a cloth dampened with water and a few drops of dishwashing liquid.

Common Surfaces

When Franck Lauret of Poitiers, France, squeegeed three 45-inch square panes (plus sills) in 12.09 seconds at the 2007 International Window Cleaning Association contest, you can bet someone in the crowd asked, "Does he do walls and carpets, too?" Because when the surfaces in your home—from popcorn ceilings to hardwood floors—require attention, you can't help wanting a speedy yet thorough fix. Fortunately, the following tactics for tackling household surfaces provide just that. Go ahead—kick some glass.

Ceilings

Out of sight, out of mind? Dust and dirt don't forget about your ceilings, even if you do. Use a drop cloth to shield furniture, then reach for the sky.

Acoustic Tile

▪ While standing on a ladder, wipe the Styrofoam-based tiles with a dry-cleaning sponge in long, smooth strokes, going in the same direction on each tile. (Short strokes will show smudges.) Don't use water; it can stain tiles.

▪ Spray a cloth with all-purpose cleaner and wipe down the metal dividers.

Painted

ENAMEL, GLOSS, AND SEMIGLOSS

▪ Dust the entire area with an extendable duster in long strokes or vacuum it on a low setting with a brush attachment. Work from the outside of the room in. Be careful of cobwebs—pull them down, as opposed to sweeping them across. Rubbing them into the wall may leave a mark.

▪ Remove greasy splatters on kitchen ceilings with a degreaser (available at hardware stores) applied to a cloth. Follow the package instructions.

FLAT LATEX

▪ Follow the advice above, omitting the degreaser. Instead, gently rub kitchen grease with a dry-cleaning sponge to remove it.

Popcorn and Texturized

▪ First, make sure your ceilings do not contain asbestos, a toxic mineral fiber used before the 1980s. (Asbestos has since been banned by the Environmental Protection Agency.) If you have any doubt, send a small sample to an EPA-certified testing laboratory. (Follow the directions for making a sample at www.epa.gov/asbestos/pubs/ashome.html, then find labs in your area certified by the National Voluntary Laboratory Accreditation Program at ts.nist.gov/standards/scopes/plmtm.htm.) Clean only nonasbestos ceilings.

▪ Dust the fragile surface with an extendable duster using long strokes, from the outside of the room in. Forgo cleaners; the kernels can disintegrate.

Wood Beams

▪ Dust beams in long strokes with an extendable cobweb brush (sold at home-improvement centers). The brush's plastic bristles won't snag on wood.

▪ For the painted portion of the ceiling, follow the advice above.

(To learn how to get stains out of ceilings, see page 107.)

CLEANING FAMOUS CEILINGS

What you need to clean your home's ceilings: a long-handled dust mop. What you need to work in the rafters of these buildings: probably an advanced degree.

▪ The constellation ceiling of Grand Central Terminal, in New York City, collected 50 years' worth of tobacco smoke before it was cleaned in 1998. Conservators vacuumed parts and used cotton cloths dipped in cleaning solution to wipe one-yard sections.

▪ Sullied by candle smoke and layers of glue meant to preserve it, Michelangelo's ceiling fresco in the Sistine Chapel required a 15-year sponge bath—from 1979 to 1994—to regain its multicolored glory.

▪ The frescoed ceiling of the Capitol Rotunda, in Washington, D.C., was dabbed with sponges soaked in water. The 1987 restoration took one year.

Walls

If your walls could talk, they'd tell tales of grimy handprints and scuff marks. Here's how to close that chapter and give walls a new beginning.

Baseboards, Moldings, Wainscoting, and Wood Paneling

PAINTED

- Dust wood with a duster or a vacuum on a low setting with a brush wand.
- Dampen a cloth with water and dishwashing liquid, wring it out well, and wipe down the surface. (Too much water can make wood warp.) Buff dry.

UNPAINTED

- Dust as directed above, and when wood looks dull, apply a wood cleaner (sold at hardware stores), following the package instructions.

Painted Surfaces

ENAMEL, GLOSS, AND SEMIGLOSS

- Dust the wall with an extendable duster, working in four-foot square sections, in long, vertical strokes from left to right and from top to bottom.
- Fill a bucket with lukewarm water. Mix 20 ounces of water and one tablespoon of dishwashing liquid in a spray bottle. Mist the solution on a wall section and wipe drips with a cloth. Let sit for five minutes to penetrate.
- Dip a sponge in the water, wring it out well, and wipe the section, using the dusting method. Rinse the sponge and repeat until you've covered the wall.
- Wipe dry with a clean cloth.

FLAT LATEX

- Wipe a four-foot square section of wall with a dry-cleaning sponge in long, vertical strokes, from top to bottom. Repeat until the entire wall is clean.

Switch Plates

- Smooth a disinfecting wipe over the surface.
- If grime builds up around the switches, dip a cotton swab in rubbing alcohol, pinch off the excess liquid with your finger, and circle the crevices.

Wallpapered Surfaces

FABRIC AND PAPER

- Vacuum on a low setting with a brush wand in four-foot square sections.

PLASTIC AND VINYL

- Follow the advice for enamel paint. Use little liquid; wallpaper can buckle.

(To learn how to remove stains from walls, see page 107.)

WORK IT OUT

The rewards of cleaning extend beyond shiny faucets. You may, in fact, tone your triceps in the process. Read on.

Washing walls: Washing and wringing movements tighten muscles in the chest and the forearms. Climbing a ladder works the quadriceps and the glutes (the same way stair machines at the gym do).

Sweeping ceilings: Think of that broom as a barbell. Lifting and pulling strengthen the upper body.

Scrubbing the bathtub: Pushing a cloth around the inside of the tub works almost every muscle in the upper body: forearms, biceps, triceps, shoulders, pectorals, and deltoids. The more soap scum, the better (at least for burning calories).

Mopping floors: A full-body workout, mopping exercises arms, legs, abdominals, and the back.

Cleaning a refrigerator: Squatting to get into shelves and bins works the legs. The only danger? Eating on the job.

Windows

Save this task for a cloudy day—glass cleaner can dry too quickly in sunshine, leaving streaks. A drop cloth will keep floors safe from falling spray.

Frames and Sills

- Open the window so you can reach the entire frame. Vacuum on high power with a brush attachment. Reach corners with a crevice attachment.
- Spray all-purpose cleaner on a cloth and wipe frames, sills, and hardware.

Glass

- Drape an old towel or sheet along the sill to protect the sill from cleaner.
- If you have decals stuck to a window, dollop regular mayonnaise on the spot, then scrape it off with an old credit card. The oils in the mayo dissolve the adhesive, and the card won't scratch the glass.
- Spray glass cleaner on the glass from top to bottom. Or pump one squirt of dishwashing liquid in a spray bottle filled with water and spritz on glass.
- Squeegee the solution off the pane from left to right, going from top to bottom in horizontal rows. No squeegee? Spray glass cleaner on a crumpled piece of newspaper and wipe, using the squeegee technique.
- If the pane is still cloudy, mix one part white vinegar and one part warm water in a spray bottle, mist it on the glass, and squeegee as above.
- Dry immediately with a cloth in horizontal strokes to avoid streaking.
- Repeat on the other side of the glass.

Painted and Stained Glass

- Sweep dust out of delicate areas with a clean, soft-bristle paintbrush.
- Wipe the glass with a cloth slightly dampened with warm water. Don't use ammonia- or vinegar-based cleaners, since they can discolor the finish.
- Dry carefully with a soft, lint-free cloth.

Screens

- Remove the screens, if possible, and vacuum both sides on a low setting with a brush attachment. Or hose them down outside with warm water.

Skylights

- If the skylight is at a dangerous height, hire a pro. (See Resources, page 117.)
- If it's easily accessible, follow the method for cleaning glass, above.

PEOPLE IN GLASS HOUSES...

...shouldn't throw stones. Or skimp on squeegees. Here's how two glass skyscrapers get clean.

- Chicago's 110-story Sears Tower has six custom window-washing machines, each designed to clean a particular facade. Manned by two engineers and loaded with washing fluid and squeegees, the machines run on tracks along the building's face.
- The tallest building in Florida, Miami's 70-story Four Seasons Hotel and Tower, is cleaned in three sections. With the help of two machines that go up and down the building, two workers armed with squeegees and one gallon of glass cleaner spend six hours, six times a year, washing the windows on the bottom section. The top two sections are cleaned twice a year.

Window Coverings

The view to the garden is lovely, but the dingy curtains framing it? Not a pretty picture. Here, cleaning steps for every blind, drape, shade, and shutter.

Blinds

CANVAS, COTTON, AND TREATED FABRICS

- Vacuum vertical blinds on a low setting with a brush wand in long strokes.
- Check the tag (usually near the back hem) for cleaning instructions. Most blinds can be submerged in a tub of a few inches of cool water and two teaspoons of dishwashing liquid. Take out the metal weights first; they can rust.
- While they're in the tub, jiggle the blinds for 5 to 10 minutes to remove dirt.
- Drain the tub, refill with several inches of clean water, and jiggle again.
- Remove the blinds and lay them on a white or colorfast towel to dry.

FAUX-WOOD AND VINYL MINI BLINDS

- Place a fabric-softener sheet between your thumb and forefinger and glide it along the top and bottom of the slats.

LINEN, SILK, AND WOOL

- Gently rub vertical blinds with a dry-cleaning sponge, using long, even strokes from top to bottom. Or have them dry-cleaned.

METAL MINI BLINDS

- Follow the advice for faux-wood mini blinds, omitting the fabric-softener sheet and instead using a cloth dampened with water and a few drops of dishwashing liquid.

WOODEN

- Vacuum blinds on a low setting with a brush attachment from left to right.
- Dampen a cloth with water and a few drops of dishwashing liquid, wring it out, and smooth it over the slats, using the method for faux-wood mini blinds.
- Dry as you go with a clean cloth. If the blinds get too wet, they could warp.

Curtains and Draperies

COTTON, POLYESTER, RAYON, AND WOOL

- Vacuum the fronts and backs of panels on a low setting by pulling a brush attachment down the fabric from top to bottom.
- If the fabric is soiled, check the label (usually located near the back hem) for cleaning instructions. Some can be machine washed on a delicate cycle.

LACE, LINEN, SATIN, AND SILK

- Vacuum on a low setting as directed above, but hold the brush wand one inch away from the fabric to avoid stretching it.
- If the curtains are dirty, have them dry-cleaned.

CLEANING 40-FOOT CURTAINS

It's a wonder that when the curtain falls at the theater, the orchestra pit doesn't let out a collective sneeze. The massive velour curtains in movie and Broadway theaters can be more than 40 feet long and are often full of dust. Because they must be flameproofed every three years by law, washing in between is out of the question. (Cleaning disables the flameproofing.) So once every three years, before they are flameproofed, the curtains are placed in large drum vats (similar to oversize washing machines) measuring about seven feet high and four feet in diameter and dry-cleaned using a petroleum-based solvent. Massive panels sometimes have to be cut in half, cleaned separately, then sewn back together. To avoid all those theatrics, workers often pound the dust off instead of sending soiled curtains out for cleaning.

Window Coverings (continued)

Curtains and Draperies

SHEER

- Blow away dust with a hair dryer on a cool, low setting, held one inch away from the fabric, moving up and down. The dryer won't overheat this fabric.
- If the curtains are dirty, have them dry-cleaned.

Shades

BAMBOO AND WOVEN WOOD

- Dampen a cloth with distilled water and wipe the shade in long strokes.
- Dry with a clean cloth.

CANVAS, COTTON, AND TREATED FABRICS

- Vacuum on a low setting with a brush attachment in vertical strokes.
- Double-check the tag (usually near the back hem) for cleaning instructions. Most shades can be cleaned using the method for canvas blinds (see previous page). Don't drown wood or metal mounts; they may get damaged.

LINEN, SILK, AND WOOL

- Gently rub the shade with a dry-cleaning sponge, using vertical strokes.

PLEATED AND ROMAN

- Dust with an extendable duster from top to bottom.
- Before cleaning, consult the care guide that came with the shades. Most can be wiped with a cloth dampened with water and dishwashing liquid.

SOLAR

- Dust with a dry microfiber cloth from top to bottom.
- Before cleaning, consult the care guide that came with the shades. Most can be wiped with a cloth dampened with distilled water.

Shutters

- Whether the plantation shutters are painted or unfinished, flip the slats up and vacuum on a low setting with a brush attachment from left to right.
- Flip the slats down and repeat the technique above.
- Dampen a cloth with water and a few drops of dishwashing liquid, wring it out, and wipe the slats and the framework, first on one side, then the other.
- Dry as you go with a clean cloth. If the wood gets too wet, it could warp.

(To learn how to remove stains from fabrics, see page 103.)

GREEN DRY-CLEAN
The upside of dry-cleaning curtains: less labor. The downside: Chemicals used in dry cleaning contaminate the earth's soil and water. The middle ground is wet cleaning, a process offered by some dry cleaners that uses water and less abrasive detergents to clean and brighten fabrics. Wet cleaning works best on water-based stains (dry cleaning generally targets oil-based stains), so it's ideal for window treatments that have been soiled by dirt and debris from the air (rather than slipcovers spotted by greasy Chinese food). When asking whether your cleaner offers wet cleaning, make sure she doesn't refer to it as "laundering," which is essentially just using a washing machine. One caveat: This process works best on polyester fabrics, since cotton, moiré, and organza can shrink by about 10 percent.

Floors

You walk, dance, and play on your floors—and track in dirt and spill things. Follow these ground rules for spotless surfaces that will floor even you.

Concrete

- Vacuum the floor on a high setting with a brush attachment, working from the left to the right corner, from the far edge to the entrance, to lift dirt.
- Squeeze a bit of dishwashing liquid into a bucket of water and plunge in a mop. Wipe the mop back and forth over a six-foot square section.
- Dip the mop into a pail of clean water and squeeze out the excess water. Repeat the technique above. Do not use abrasive cleansers, ammonia, or nonchlorine bleach, which can scratch or fade the finish.

Cork

- Follow the advice for concrete floors, above, but wring the mop out well before using it. Too much moisture on cork can seep into the edges and cause buckling.
- If the surface still looks grimy, squirt dishwashing liquid onto a mop and scrub back and forth over the surface. Rinse with a barely damp mop.

Hardwood

NONURETHANED HARD FINISHES (LACQUERED AND SHELLACKED)

- Vacuum on high power with a brush attachment, working from the left to the right corner, from the far edge to the entrance. Do not use water, which can stain the wood and seep in between slats, causing the wood to buckle.

POLYURETHANED HARD FINISHES

- Vacuum on high power with a brush attachment, using the technique above. Vacuuming is the recommended cleaning method because liquid can foster mold and mildew and cause planks to buckle or form bumps. Avoid using a hard-bristle broom, which can scratch the finish.
- If the floor looks dull after vacuuming, wet a cloth with warm water and a tad of dishwashing liquid. Wring out the cloth extremely well and wipe the floor in six-foot square sections, going with the grain.
- Buff the floor with a clean cloth to lift soapy residue.
- Still not sparkling? Use a wood-floor cleaner and the method recommended by the flooring manufacturer. Don't be tempted to try sprays or oils intended for use on wood furniture; they can make a floor dangerously slippery.

ARE YOUR FLOORS WAXED?

It's important to know whether you have a waxed or a no-wax floor. After all, wood cleaners are formulated differently for each. But it's not always easy to tell these floors apart. Here are two simple ways to figure it out.

- Check the finish. Waxed floors are glossy; no-wax floors look dull.
- Spot-check the floor. Apply a small amount of mineral spirits to a white cloth and dab the floor in a low-traffic area. If a slight yellow or brown color appears on the cloth, you most likely have a paste-wax finish. To test for an acrylic wax, mix a solution of equal parts dish soap, ammonia, and water and rub a small amount on the floor in a low-traffic area. If the spot turns white, you have an acrylic-wax finish.

Floors (continued)

Linoleum

- Vacuum the floor on a high setting with a brush wand, working from the left to the right corner, from the far edge to the entrance. Or use a dust mop.
- Dilute a squirt of dishwashing liquid in a bucket of water, dip in a mop, and wipe the mop back and forth over the floor in six-foot square sections.
- Plunge the mop into a pail of clean water, squeeze out the excess water, and repeat the technique above.

Plastic Laminates (Such as Alloc, Mohawk, and Pergo)

- Vacuum on high power with a brush wand from the far edge to the entrance.
- Dilute one cup of white vinegar in a gallon of water. Dip in a mop, wring it out well, and mop the floor, using the technique for linoleum.

Stone (Granite, Limestone, Marble, Slate, and Terrazzo)

- Vacuum on high power with a brush wand from the far edge to the entrance.
- Squeeze a bit of dishwashing liquid into a bucket of warm water. Dunk in a mop, wring it out, and mop the floor, using the linoleum technique. Do not use abrasives, ammonia, or bleach, all of which can damage stone.
- Buff with a clean cloth to shine.

Tile

GLAZED CERAMIC

- Vacuum on high power with a brush wand from the far edge to the entrance.
- Mix one capful of rubbing alcohol with one gallon of water. Dip a mop in the solution and mop the floor, using the technique for linoleum. Avoid oil soaps and ammonia, which yellow grout, and vinegar, which can damage it.

UNGLAZED

- Use the advice above, omitting rubbing alcohol for a squirt of dish soap.

Vinyl

- Vacuum on high power with a brush wand from the far edge to the entrance.
- Mix ½ cup of ammonia with one gallon of water. Mop the floor, using the linoleum technique. Don't use detergents, which leave a film behind.

(To find out how to remove tricky stains from floors, see page 109.)

(To find out how to remove tricky stains from floors, see page 109.)

ECO-FRIENDLY FLOORING

Having a hard time getting excited about hardwood? These three green floors are all easy to clean.

- Bamboo, the fastest-growing plant, is beautiful and renewable. It can be harvested every four to six years (versus 30 to 50 years for typical hard-wood trees), and it can be cleaned with a dust mop.
- Reclaimed-wood floors are made of tim-ber from fallen trees and wood salvaged from buildings. A damp mop is all that's needed to clean the floor's planks.
- Recycled-glass tiles are made from discarded glass, which is melted down and crafted into tiles by artisans. They look delicate but are durable: The tiles resist stains and can be wiped clean with dishwashing liquid. (For eco-friendly flooring sources, go to www.thegreenguide.com.)

Carpets and Rugs

A lot can hide in your carpets, including, perhaps, that earring you lost in 2001. Bring it all to the surface (and vacuum it up) with these guidelines.

Antique, Delicate, and Oriental Rugs

- Sweep the carpet and the fringe with a nylon-bristle broom. Don't vacuum—suction can loosen fibers from the weave. Water and cleaners can stain.
- Hire a specialist to do the cleaning, if necessary. (See Resources, page 117.)

Natural Fibers (Coir, Sea Grass, Sisal, and Wool)

CARPETS

- Vacuum the carpet on high power with a brush attachment, starting at the far left corner of the room and working your way to the right, then out of the room. To remove ground-in dirt, push the vacuum back and forth over low-traffic spots four times; seven times over high-traffic areas.
- Dampen a cloth with water and blot soiled areas. (Cleaners can stain.)
- Blot with a dry towel.
- Allow to air-dry.
- Hire a professional to shampoo the carpet. (See Resources, page 117.)

RUGS

- Place the rug facedown on a clean old sheet to protect the floor from dirt and vacuum on a low setting with a rug or brush attachment or a beater bar.
- Flip the rug over onto a clean spot of the floor. Fold up the sheet.
- Repeat the vacuuming instructions above to clean the topside of the rug.
- Follow the advice above for cleaning soiled areas.

Synthetics (Nylon, Polyester, and Polypropylene)

CARPETS

- Vacuum and spot-treat with water as directed for natural-fiber carpets. Synthetics often have a stain-resistant coating, so you don't need cleaner.
- Blot treated spots with a dry towel.
- Gently scrub damp areas with a soft, clean carpet brush to raise the pile and expose the fibers to the air so they dry more quickly.
- Hire a professional to deep-clean. (See Resources, page 117.) Don't rent a steam cleaner; machines can leave too much moisture, resulting in mildew.

RUGS

- Follow the advice above for cleaning natural-fiber rugs.

(To learn how to remove stains from carpets, turn to page 111.)

RED CARPET READY

Vacuuming isn't very glamorous. But a carpet can be—if it's the red carpet at the Academy Awards. Once a year, the same 33-by-500-foot hunk of carpet is rolled out to welcome Hollywood's well-heeled. It comes complete with its own designer label—"Cayenne," the name of its custom dye color. Adoring fans? How about a crew of 20 that installs the carpet's many sections in five days? The process is taken so seriously that only workers who have been with the company for at least one year are allowed to install the carpet. On awards-show day, it receives one last vacuuming. After the show, it is steam-cleaned, then placed in storage. Dirty or worn pieces are thrown away and replaced. Out with the old, in with the new. Sounds like show business.

Stains

Picasso, your three-year-old is not. Otherwise, her scribbles on the wall would be worth a fortune. But before you hastily take sponge to painted wall, think outside the (crayon) box and try these simple methods for removing the most common stains from the most common materials in your home. Find your stained surface, scroll down to the offending stain, glance at the corresponding list of cleaner solutions, and complete the steps in order, stopping as soon as the stain is gone. Finally, you've hit pay dirt.

All-purpose cleaner:
Spray a cloth with
all-purpose cleaner.
Ammonia: Mix one tablespoon of clear ammonia
with one cup of water.
Wet a cloth; wring it out.
Baking soda: Mix one
teaspoon of baking soda
with one teaspoon of
water. Smear on a cloth.
Bleach: Combine three
parts bleach with one
part warm water. Wet a
cloth and wring it out.
Denatured alcohol:
Wet a cloth with dena-
tured alcohol (available
at hardware stores).
Detergent: Dilute ½
teaspoon of dish soap in
two cups of water. Wet a
cloth and wring it out.
Hydrogen peroxide:
Pour hydrogen peroxide
on a cloth. Wring it out.
Rubbing alcohol:
Wet a cloth with rubbing
alcohol. Wring it out.
Mineral oil: Pour mineral
oil on a cloth. Wring it out.
Rust remover: Pour rust
remover (sold at hard-
ware stores) on a cloth.
Vinegar: Mix one cup
each of vinegar and water.
Wet a cloth; wring it out.

Surfaces

To remove the most common stains found on each surface, use the
following strategies and solutions (see Solutions for Surfaces, left).

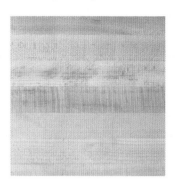

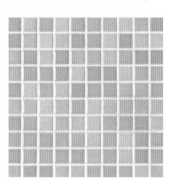

Butcher Block

**Butter, Coffee, Cooking Oil, Juice,
Ketchup, Mayonnaise, Milk, Salad
Dressing, Soda, Tea, Wine:** Blot
with detergent solution. Rub
half of a cut lemon on the
stain.

Ink, Permanent Felt-Tip Marker:
Blot with rubbing-alcohol
solution. Sprinkle scouring
powder on the spot and scrub
with a sponge. Rub half of a
cut lemon on the spot. Blot
with mineral-oil solution.

Water Marks: Rub with mineral-
oil solution.

Wax: Fill a plastic bag with ice
and place it on top of the wax.
When the wax is hard, shatter
the spot with a butter knife.
Scrape up the chips with a
putty knife or an old credit
card. Apply detergent solution. Rub the stain with half of
a cut lemon.

Ceramic Tile

**Butter, Ketchup, Mayonnaise, Nail
Polish, Salad Dressing:** Blot with
detergent solution. Apply a
degreaser (sold at hardware
stores) to the spot. Wipe with a
damp cloth. Use a premade
poultice (sold at stone dealers).

Coffee, Tea: Pour a few drops of
both ammonia and hydrogen
peroxide on the stain. When it
stops bubbling, blot with a
damp cloth. Use a premade
poultice (at stone dealers).

Mildew, Mold: Scrub with baking-
soda solution.

Milk: Blot with detergent solution, then bleach solution. Wipe
with a cloth. Use a premade
poultice (at stone dealers).

Rust: Scrub with rust-remover
solution. Wipe with a damp
cloth. Use a premade poultice
(sold at stone dealers).

Wine: Pour acetone on stain.
Blot with a dry cloth. Repeat.

Linoleum

Butter, Coffee, Cooking Oil, Juice, Ketchup, Mayonnaise, Milk, Nail Polish, Salad Dressing, Soda, Tea, Wine: Blot with all-purpose cleaner solution. Wipe with a damp cloth.

Mildew, Mold: Blot stain with hydrogen peroxide solution.

Rust: Sprinkle salt on half of a cut lemon and rub into stain. Wipe with a damp cloth.

Wax: Fill a plastic bag with ice and place it on top of the wax. When the wax is hard, shatter the spot with a butter knife. Spray all-purpose cleaner on a nylon scrubber and rub the spot. Wipe with a damp cloth.

Plastic Laminate (Such as Formica)

Butter, Coffee, Cooking Oil, Juice, Ketchup, Mayonnaise, Mildew, Milk, Mold, Nail Polish, Salad Dressing, Soda, Tea, Wine: Consult the manufacturer's care guide for advice. You can blot most brands with baking-soda solution. Wipe with a damp cloth. Blot with a dry cloth.

Wax: Fill a plastic bag with ice and place it on top of the wax. When the wax is hard, shatter the spot with a butter knife. Gently scrape the chips with an old credit card. Wipe with a damp cloth.

Porcelain Enamel

Hard Water: Blot with vinegar solution. Wipe with a damp cloth.

Mildew, Mold: Squirt mildly abrasive creamy cleanser on the stain and rub with a dry cloth. Wipe with a damp cloth.

Rust: Rub with rust-remover solution. Wipe with a damp cloth.

Surfaces (continued)

To remove common stains found on each surface, use the following strategies and solutions (see Solutions for Surfaces, page 100).

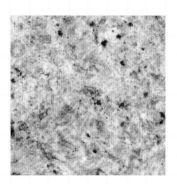

Solid Surfaces (Such as Avonite and Corian)

Butter, Cooking Oil, Lotion, Salad Dressing: Apply a degreaser (at hardware stores), following the package instructions.

Coffee, Juice, Ketchup, Mayonnaise, Milk, Soda, Tea: Blot with baking-soda solution. Wipe with a damp cloth.

Mildew, Mold: Rub with baking-soda solution. Blot with a damp cloth. Dab dry.

Rust: If matte, rub with rust-remover solution. Blot with detergent solution. Blot with a damp cloth. If high gloss, follow matte steps, using vinegar solution instead of detergent.

Wax: If matte, apply a gum-removing solvent (at hardware stores). Blot with detergent solution. Blot with a damp cloth. If high gloss, follow steps for matte, using vinegar solution instead of detergent.

Stainless Steel

Mineral Deposits: Pour a small amount of vinegar on the stain. Rub with a dry cloth.

Rust, Water Marks: Use a cleaner formulated for stainless steel (available at hardware stores), following the package instructions.

Stone (Granite, Limestone, Marble, Slate)

Butter, Lotion, Mayonnaise, Salad Dressing: Blot with detergent solution. Apply a degreaser (at hardware stores), following the package directions. Wipe with a damp cloth. Use a premade poultice (at stone dealers).

Coffee, Tea: Pour a few drops of 35 percent hydrogen peroxide on the stain, then a few drops of ammonia. When bubbling stops, blot with a damp cloth.

Mildew, Mold: Scrub stain with baking-soda solution.

Milk: Blot with detergent solution. Blot with bleach solution. Let stand for about three minutes. Wipe with a damp cloth.

Rust: Scrub with rust-remover solution. Blot with a damp cloth. Use a premade poultice.

Wine: Pour acetone on the stain and blot with a cloth. Repeat.

Upholstery

To remove the most common stains found on each fabric, use the following strategies and solutions (see Solutions for Upholstery, right).

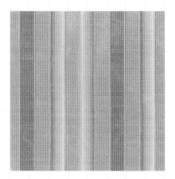

Canvas, Cotton, Linen, and Rayon

Coffee, Tea: Spray vinegar solution. Blot with a damp cloth. Spray ammonia solution. Blot with a damp cloth. Blot with a dry cloth.

Dirt, Mud: Let dry. Spray detergent solution. Blot with a damp cloth. Blot with a dry cloth.

Ink: Blot with dry-cleaning fluid. Blot with rubbing-alcohol solution. Spray detergent solution. Blot with a damp cloth. Blot with a dry cloth.

Juice, Soda: Spray detergent solution. Blot with a damp cloth. Spray ammonia solution. Blot with a damp cloth. Spray vinegar solution. Blot with a damp cloth. Dab dry.

Pet Accidents, Wine: Spray detergent solution. Blot with a damp cloth. Spray vinegar solution. Blot with a damp cloth. Blot with a dry cloth.

Chenille, Corduroy, Velvet, and Wool

Coffee, Tea: Spray vinegar solution. Blot with a damp cloth, wiping with the fabric pile. Spray ammonia solution. Blot with a damp cloth. Dab dry.

Dirt, Mud: Let dry. Spray detergent solution. Blot with a damp cloth. Blot with a dry cloth.

Ink: Blot with dry-cleaning fluid. Blot with rubbing-alcohol solution. Spray detergent solution. Blot with a damp cloth. Blot with a dry cloth.

Juice, Soda: Spray detergent solution. Blot with a damp cloth. Spray ammonia solution. Blot with a damp cloth. Spray vinegar solution. Blot with a damp cloth. Dab dry.

Pet Accidents, Wine: Spray detergent solution. Blot with a damp cloth. Spray vinegar solution. Blot with a damp cloth. Blot with a dry cloth.

SOLUTIONS FOR UPHOLSTERY

Ammonia: Mix one tablespoon of clear ammonia with one cup of water in a spray bottle.

Detergent: Combine 1/2 teaspoon of mild dishwashing liquid with two cups of lukewarm water in a spray bottle.

Dry-cleaning fluid: Squirt dry-cleaning fluid (available at home-improvement centers) onto a microfiber cloth.

Rubbing alcohol: Pour a few drops of rubbing alcohol onto a cloth.

Vinegar: Mix one cup of white vinegar and one cup of lukewarm water in a spray bottle.

Upholstery (continued)

To remove the most common stains found on each fabric, use the following strategies and solutions (see Solutions for Upholstery, page 103).

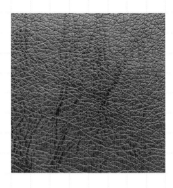

Leather and Suede

All Stains: Consult the manufacturer of the furniture and use a recommended cleaner. If that doesn't work, consult a professional. To find one in your area, search listings of the Professional Carpet and Upholstery Cleaners Association by visiting www.pcuca.org.

Jacquard and Silk

Coffee, Tea: Spray vinegar solution. Blot with a cloth. Spray ammonia solution. Blot with a damp cloth. Blot with a dry cloth.

Dirt, Mud: Let dry. Spray detergent solution. Blot with a damp cloth. Blot with a dry cloth.

Ink: Blot with dry-cleaning fluid. Blot with rubbing-alcohol solution. Spray detergent solution. Blot with a damp cloth. Blot with a dry cloth.

Juice, Soda: Spray detergent solution. Blot with a damp cloth. Spray ammonia solution. Blot with a damp cloth. Spray vinegar solution. Blot with a damp cloth. Blot with a dry cloth.

Pet Accidents, Wine: Spray detergent solution. Blot with a damp cloth. Spray vinegar solution. Blot with a damp cloth. Blot with a dry cloth.

Vinyl

Coffee, Juice, Soda, Tea, Wine: Blot with a dry cloth. Spray detergent solution. Blot with a dry cloth.

Dirt, Mud: Spray detergent solution. Blot with a dry cloth.

Ink: Blot with rubbing-alcohol solution. Blot with a dry cloth.

Pet Accidents: Blot with a dry cloth. Spray detergent solution. Blot with a dry cloth.

Furniture

To remove the most common stains found on each type, use the following strategies and solutions (see Solutions for Furniture, right).

Acrylic

All Stains: Blot with detergent solution. Blot with a damp cloth.

Hard Finishes (Lacquer, Polyurethane) and Painted Wood

Butter, Coffee, Cooking Oil, Dirt, Juice, Mud, Soda, Tea, Wine: Blot with detergent solution. Blot with wood-cleaner solution. Wipe with a damp cloth. Wipe with a dry cloth.

Ink: Blot with all-purpose cleaner solution. Wipe with a damp cloth. Wipe with a dry cloth.

Water Stains: Wipe with a cotton cloth dampened with detergent solution. Buff with a dry cloth.

Wax: Let air-dry. When the wax is hard, scrape it with an old credit card. Wipe with a damp cloth. Wipe with a dry cloth.

SOLUTIONS FOR FURNITURE

All-purpose cleaner: Spray all-purpose cleaner onto a microfiber cloth.

Baking soda: Make a paste of one teaspoon of baking soda and one teaspoon of warm water. Smear it on a cloth.

Denatured alcohol: Pour denatured alcohol (available at hardware stores) on a cloth.

Detergent: Mix 1/2 teaspoon of mild translucent dishwashing liquid with two cups of lukewarm water. Wet a microfiber cloth in the solution. Wring it out.

Furniture polish: Smear a small amount of furniture polish (available at hardware stores) onto a cloth.

Mineral spirits: Mix a solution of one part mineral spirits, one part raw linseed oil, and a dash of white vinegar. Wet a cloth in the solution.

Wood cleaner: Pour a small amount of wood cleaner (available at hardware stores) on a cloth.

Furniture (continued)

To remove the most common stains found on each type, use the following strategies and solutions (see Solutions for Furniture, page 105).

  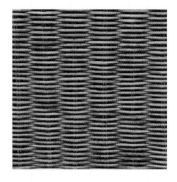

Oil Finish

Butter, Coffee, Cooking Oil, Dirt, Juice, Mud, Soda, Tea, Wine: Blot with detergent solution. Blot with wood-cleaner solution. Wipe with a damp cloth. Wipe with a dry cloth.

Ink: Blot with all-purpose cleaner solution. Wipe with a damp cloth. Dab with a dry cloth.

Water Stains: Rub mineral spirits into the wood grain with fine steel wool. Buff with a dry cloth.

Wax: Let air-dry. When the wax is hard, scrape it with an old credit card. Blot with baking-soda solution. Wipe with a damp cloth. Wipe with a dry cloth.

Shellacked or Varnished

Butter, Coffee, Cooking Oil, Dirt, Ink, Juice, Mud, Soda, Tea, Wax, Wine: Blot with furniture-polish solution.

Water Stains: Blot with mineral-spirits solution.

Wicker

Butter, Coffee, Cooking Oil, Dirt, Juice, Mud, Soda, Tea, Wine: Blot with detergent solution. Wipe with a damp cloth.

Ink: Blot with denatured-alcohol solution. Blot with detergent solution. Wipe with a damp cloth.

Wax: Fill a plastic bag with ice and place it on top of the wax. When the wax is hard, scrape off chips with a credit card. Blot with detergent solution. Wipe with a damp cloth.

Ceilings and Walls

To remove the most common stains found on each surface, use these strategies and solutions (see Solutions for Ceilings and Walls, right).

Acoustic Tile and Popcorn Ceilings

All Stains: First, check to see if your popcorn ceiling contains asbestos by following the advice on page 83. If it is asbestos-free, respray the popcorn or consult a professional to repair the spot without damaging the texture. Stained acoustic tiles can be replaced by a professional. To find a licensed contractor in your area, search the listings at www.servicemagic.com.

Painted

Butter, Coffee, Crayon, Dirt, Ink, Mud, Soda, Tea: Blot with all-purpose cleaner solution. Blot with household cleaning-powder solution. Blot with a damp cloth.

Permanent Felt-Tip Marker: Blot with denatured alcohol. Blot with detergent solution.

Scuffs: Rub with a foam sponge eraser (available at hardware and grocery stores).

SOLUTIONS FOR CEILINGS AND WALLS

All-purpose cleaner: Spray all-purpose cleaner onto a microfiber cloth.

Denatured alcohol: Pour denatured alcohol (available at hardware stores) on a cloth.

Detergent solution: Mix $1/2$ teaspoon of translucent dishwashing liquid with two cups of lukewarm water. Wet a cloth and wring it out.

Household cleaning powder: Dissolve household cleaning powder (sold at grocery stores) in a bowl of hot water, following the package instructions. Wet a sponge and wring it out well.

Wood cleaner: Pour a small amount of wood cleaner (sold at hardware stores) on a cloth.

Ceilings and Walls (continued)

To remove common stains found on each surface, use the following strategies and solutions (see Solutions for Ceilings and Walls, page 107).

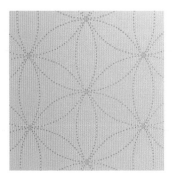

Wainscoting and Wood Paneling

Butter, Coffee, Crayon, Dirt, Ink, Mud, Soda, Tea: Blot with detergent solution. Blot with wood-cleaner solution. Wipe with a damp cloth. Dry with a cloth.

Permanent Felt-Tip Marker: Blot with all-purpose cleaner solution. Wipe with a damp cloth. Dry with a cloth.

Scuffs: Rub with a foam sponge eraser (available at hardware and grocery stores).

Wallpaper (Vinyl, Vinyl Coated)

Butter, Coffee, Crayon, Dirt, Ink, Mud, Permanent Felt-Tip Marker, Soda, Tea: Blot with detergent solution.

Smudges: Rub with a clean pencil eraser or a foam sponge eraser (available at hardware and grocery stores).

Wood Beams

Cooking Oil, Dirt, Mud: Blot with detergent solution. Blot with wood-cleaner solution. Wipe with a damp cloth. Dry with a cloth.

Floors

To remove the most common stains found on each type of floor, use the following strategies and solutions (see Solutions for Floors, right).

Cork

Chewing Gum, Wax: Fill a plastic bag with ice and place it on top of the stain. When the spot hardens, shatter it with a blunt object, such as a spatula. Scrape up the chips with a putty knife or an old credit card. Wipe with a damp cloth. Blot with bleach solution. Wipe with a damp cloth.

Coffee, Cooking Oil, Crayon, Dirt, Juice, Mud, Soda, Tea: Blot with detergent solution.

Pet Accidents: Blot with detergent solution. Blot with bleach solution. Wipe with a damp cloth.

Scuffs: Rub with a foam sponge eraser (available at hardware and grocery stores).

Hardwood (Polyurethaned)

Butter, Cooking Oil, Crayon: Blot with hydrogen peroxide solution. Blot with wood-cleaner solution. Blot with a dry cloth.

Chewing Gum, Wax: Fill a plastic bag with ice and place it on top of the stain. When the spot hardens, shatter it with a blunt object, such as a spatula. Scrape up the chips with a putty knife or an old credit card. Blot with wood-cleaner solution. Blot with a dry cloth.

Coffee, Dirt, Juice, Mud, Soda, Tea: Blot with wood-cleaner solution. Blot with a dry cloth.

Pet Accidents: Blot with wood-cleaner solution. Blot with hydrogen peroxide solution. Blot with a dry cloth.

Scuffs: Rub with a foam sponge eraser (available at hardware and grocery stores).

Floors (continued)

To remove common stains found on each type of floor, use the following strategies and solutions (see Solutions for Floors, page 109).

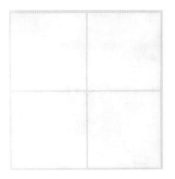 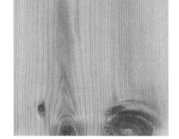 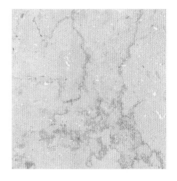

Linoleum and Vinyl

Butter, Coffee, Cooking Oil, Crayon, Dirt, Juice, Mud, Pet Accidents, Soda, Tea: Blot with all-purpose cleaner solution. Wipe with a damp cloth.

Chewing Gum, Wax: Fill a plastic bag with ice and place it on the stain. When the stain hardens, shatter it with a butter knife or a spatula. Scrape up the chips with a putty knife or an old credit card. Scrub with all-purpose cleaner solution spritzed on a nylon scrubber (available at hardware stores), instead of a cloth. Wipe with a damp cloth.

Scuffs: Rub with a foam sponge eraser (available at hardware and grocery stores).

Plastic Laminate (Such as Mohawk and Pergo)

Butter, Coffee, Cooking Oil, Crayon, Dirt, Juice, Mud, Pet Accidents, Soda, Tea: Apply the cleaner recommended by the floor manufacturer, following the package instructions.

Chewing Gum, Wax: Fill a plastic bag with ice and place it on top of the stain. When the stain hardens, shatter it with a butter knife or a spatula. Scrape up the chips with a putty knife or an old credit card. Apply the cleaner recommended by the manufacturer, following the package instructions.

Scuffs: Rub with a foam sponge eraser (available at hardware and grocery stores).

Stone (Granite, Limestone, Marble, Slate) and Tile

Butter: Blot with detergent solution. Apply a degreaser (available at hardware stores). Wipe with a damp cloth.

Chewing Gum, Wax: Fill a plastic bag with ice and place it on top of the stain. When the stain hardens, scrape it with a credit card. Dab with a dry spotter (at janitor-supply stores).

Coffee, Tea: Pour a few drops of both hydrogen peroxide and ammonia on the stain. (It will bubble.) Blot with a cloth.

Pet Accidents: Blot with vinegar solution. Apply a bacteria and enzyme digester (at janitor-supply stores) to a cloth and blot. Wipe with a damp cloth.

Scuffs: Rub with a foam sponge eraser (at hardware stores).

Wine: Pour acetone on stain and blot with a cloth. Repeat.

Carpets

To remove the most common stains found on each type of carpet, use the following strategies and solutions (see Solutions for Carpets, right).

Natural Fibers
(Coir, Jute, Sisal, Wool)

Butter, Crayon, Ink, Permanent Felt-Tip Marker: Blot with oil-solvent solution. Spray detergent solution. Blot with a damp cloth. Let dry. Repeat steps.

Chewing Gum, Wax: Fill a plastic bag with ice and rub on the spot until it hardens. Shatter the spot. Vacuum the chips. Blot with oil-solvent solution. Dab with a damp cloth.

Coffee, Dirt, Mud, Tea: Spray detergent solution. Blot with a cloth. Spray vinegar solution. Blot. Repeat detergent solution. Blot with a damp cloth.

Ink, Juice, Pet Accidents, Soda, Wine: Spray detergent solution and blot with a cloth. Spray ammonia solution and blot. Spray vinegar solution and blot. Repeat detergent solution. Spray water and blot with a dry cloth. Repeat steps.

Synthetic Fibers
(Nylon, Polyester)

Butter, Crayon, Ink, Permanent Felt-Tip Marker: Blot with oil-solvent solution. Spray water and blot with a dry cloth. Let dry. Repeat steps.

Chewing Gum, Wax: Fill a plastic bag with ice and rub on the spot until it hardens. Shatter the spot with a blunt object. Vacuum the chips. Blot with oil-solvent solution. Dab with a damp cloth.

Coffee, Juice, Pet Accidents, Soda, Tea, Wine: Blot with detergent solution. Wait 15 minutes. Blot with a dry cloth. Blot with vinegar solution. Wait 15 minutes. Blot with a damp cloth. Let dry. Repeat steps.

Dirt, Mud: Vacuum dry dirt. Blot with detergent solution. Wait 15 minutes. Blot with a damp cloth.

SOLUTIONS FOR NATURAL-FIBER CARPETS

Ammonia: Mix one tablespoon of clear household ammonia with 1/2 cup of lukewarm water in a spray bottle.

Detergent: Mix one teaspoon of dishwashing liquid with one cup of water in a spray bottle.

Oil solvent: Apply a small amount of oil solvent, such as nonacetone nail-polish remover, to a cloth.

Vinegar: Mix 1/4 cup of white vinegar and 1/4 cup of water in a spray bottle.

SOLUTIONS FOR SYNTHETIC-FIBER CARPETS

Detergent: Mix 1/4 teaspoon of dishwashing liquid with one cup of lukewarm water. Wet a cloth and wring it out.

Oil solvent: Apply a bit of oil solvent, such as nonacetone nail-polish remover, to a cloth.

Vinegar: Add one cup of white vinegar to two cups of water. Wet a cloth and wring it out.

Reference Guide

Things you must commit to memory: your ATM PIN, your computer log-in, your Social Security number. So with precious mental real estate devoted to PINs and passwords, how are you supposed to remember how often to clean the stove hood or the phone number of that miracle-working carpet cleaner? With the timeline of important tasks and the list of resources on the following pages, you'll have everything you need at your fingertips. As for trying to commit it all to memory? Forget about it.

Cleaning Calendar

When your chores seem utterly insurmountable, use this handy periodic table of important cleaning tasks (color-coded by how often they should be completed) to stay on top of everything.

Fu FURNITURE Dust all hard surfaces.	**Toi** TOILET Scrub and disinfect.				
Fl FLOORS Vacuum or mop.	**Sk** KITCHEN SINK Scrub and disinfect.	**U** UPHOLSTERY Vacuum.	**Bu** STOVE BURNER GRATES Scrub clean.	**C-w** CURTAINS (WASHABLE) Launder or hand wash.	
Ap APPLIANCES Wipe down surfaces.	**Shw** SHOWER Clean and scrub down.	**Wb** WASTEBASKETS Wipe out and disinfect.	**Mg** MOLDINGS Dust.	**Mt** MATTRESSES Vacuum every 3 months; flip every 6.	**Dr** DRAPES Deep-vacuum.
Cn COUNTERS Wipe down and disinfect.	**Tu** BATHTUB Clean and scrub down.	**Dk** DOORKNOBS Wipe down and disinfect.	**Kc** KITCHEN CABINETS Wipe down.	**Fu-l** FURNITURE (LEATHER) Clean and condition.	**Bb** BASEBOARDS Wash or wipe down.
	Sh SHEETS Change and launder.	**Cf** CEILING FANS Wipe off and dust.	**Mi** MICROWAVE Clean and deodorize.	**Bl-w** BLINDS (WOODEN) Wash.	**Wi** WINDOWS Wash inside and out.

R
RUGS
Professionally clean.

Hd
STOVE HOOD
Clean and degrease.

Sc
SLIPCOVERS
Wash or dry-clean.

Cb
CABINETS
Empty and clean.

U-u
UPHOLSTERY (UNWASHABLE)
Have cleaned every 2 years.

Wa
WALLS
Wash.

Ap-s
APPLIANCES (STAINLESS STEEL)
Polish.

O
OVEN
Clean.

Pw
PILLOWS
Launder or dry-clean.

Gr
TILE GROUT
Scrub.

Car
CARPETING
Professionally clean.

Py
PANTRY
Clean thoroughly.

Re
REFRIGERATOR
Clean interior.

Ls
LAMP SHADES
Wash and clean.

Cm
COMFORTER
Launder or dry-clean.

Cc
CONDENSER COIL (REFRIGERATOR)
Vacuum or dust.

Fs
FABRIC SHADES
Professionally clean every 2 years.

Dr
DRAPES
Professionally clean every 2 years.

Cff
COFFEEMAKER
Clean and descale.

U-w
UPHOLSTERY (WASHABLE)
Sponge-clean.

Fs-w
FABRIC SHADES (WASHABLE)
Wash.

Fi
FILTER (STOVE HOOD)
Wash and dry.

Fl-w
WOOD FLOORS (POLYURETHANED)
Touch up as needed.

THE KEY: ▮ WEEKLY ▮ MONTHLY ▮ EVERY 3 TO 6 MONTHS ▮ EVERY 6 TO 12 MONTHS ▮ EVERY YEAR OR SO

115

Resources

By now, you're somewhat of a cleaning expert. For the (few) answers you don't have and the tasks you can't complete alone, here's where to turn.

Air Quality

- **Asthma and Allergy Foundation of America**
Call the hotline or search the site to access information on prevention and treatment.
PHONE: 800-727-8462; weekdays, 10 A.M. to 3 P.M. ET.
WEBSITE: www.aafa.org.

- **U.S. Environmental Protection Agency Indoor Air Quality**
Speak to an information specialist about air pollution or search the A-to-Z index of indoor air-quality issues.
PHONE: 202-343-9370; weekdays, 8 A.M. to 5 P.M. ET.
WEBSITE: www.epa.gov/iaq.

Cleaning Services

CARPET CLEANERS

- **Carpet and Rug Institute**
Search lists of manufacturer-recommended pros and certified cleaning products.
WEBSITE: www.carpet-rug.org.

- **Institute of Inspection, Cleaning, and Restoration Certification**
Search for a firm near you.
PHONE: 800-835-4624; weekdays, 9 A.M. to 8 P.M. ET.
WEBSITE: www.certified cleaners.org.

CHIMNEY SWEEPS

- **Chimney Safety Institute of America**
Search by state to locate a certified sweeper.
PHONE: 317-837-5362; weekdays, 8 A.M. to 5 P.M. ET.
WEBSITE: www.csia.org.

- **Hearth, Patio & Barbecue Association**
Search by ZIP code for local professionals.
WEBSITE: www.hpba.org.

DAMAGE CLEANUP

- **ServiceMaster Clean**
Search by ZIP code for a professional to restore your home and furnishings after water, fire, or smoke damage.
PHONE: 800-633-5703; weekdays, 8 A.M. to 5 P.M. CT.
WEBSITE: www.servicemaster clean.com.

HARDWOOD-FLOOR CLEANERS

- **National Wood Flooring Association**
Type in your ZIP code or city for a list of professionals in your area.
PHONE: 800-422-4556; weekdays, 8 A.M. to 5 P.M. CT.
WEBSITE: www.woodfloors.org/ consumer/findpro.aspx.

HOUSECLEANING SERVICES

- **Merry Maids**
Search for a local franchise.
PHONE: 800-798-8000; 24 hours a day.
WEBSITE: www.merrymaids.com.

- **The Maids**
Search for a local franchise.
PHONE: 800-843-6243; 24 hours a day.
WEBSITE: www.maids.com.

UPHOLSTERY CLEANERS

- **Professional Carpet and Upholstery Cleaners Association**
Browse an extensive list of company names to find contact information for a licensed upholstery cleaner in your area.
WEBSITE: www.pcuca.org.

WINDOW CLEANERS

- **International Window Cleaning Association**
Search by state or company name to locate a certified professional who specializes in washing skylights or oversize windows.
PHONE: 800-875-4922; weekdays, 8:30 A.M. to 5:30 P.M. CT.
WEBSITE: www.iwca.org.

Emergency Contacts

HEALTH AND SAFETY

- **Centers for Disease Control and Prevention** Browse the A-to-Z index of bacterial infections for information on prevention, diagnosis, and treatment. Or call for information. PHONE: 800-311-3435; weekdays, 8 A.M. to 4:30 P.M. ET. WEBSITE: www.cdc.gov/az.do.
- **Food Safety and Inspection Service of the United States Department of Agriculture** Download fact sheets on safe food handling and emergency preparedness. Or call the hotline with food-safety questions. PHONE: 888-674-6854; weekdays, 10 A.M. to 4 P.M. ET. WEBSITE: www.fsis.usda.gov.

POISON CONTROL CENTERS

- **American Association of Poison Control Centers** Read poison-prevention tips and search to locate a poison control center in your area. Or call the hotline for help during emergencies. PHONE: 800-222-1222; 24 hours a day. WEBSITE: www.aapcc.org.

- **American Society for the Prevention of Cruelty to Animals** Call the hotline if your pet accidentally ingests a cleaning product. PHONE: 888-426-4435; 24 hours a day. WEBSITE: www.aspca.org.

Pest Control

- **National Pest Management Association** Type in your ZIP code for a list of pest professionals in your area. WEBSITE: www.pestworld.org.
- **National Pesticide Information Center** Browse advice about choosing a pest-control company. PHONE: 800-858-7378; daily, 6:30 A.M. to 4:30 P.M. PT. WEBSITE: www.npic.orst.edu.

Products and Tools

ECO-FRIENDLY BRANDS

- **Conscious Consumer Marketplace of the Center for a New American Dream** Find companies that sell eco-friendly goods. PHONE: 877-683-7326; weekdays, 9 A.M. to 5 P.M. ET. WEBSITE: www.newdream.org.

- **Green Seal** Search recommendations of cleaning products. WEBSITE: www.greenseal.org.

HOUSEHOLD CLEANERS

- **Household Products Database of the U.S. National Library of Medicine** Browse through entries for 6,000 brand-name cleaning products for label information and ingredients. WEBSITE: www.household products.nlm.nih.gov.

PRODUCT SAFETY

- **U.S. Consumer Product Safety Commission** Report an unsafe product or tool and get informed about recent recalls and product-safety news. PHONE: 800-638-2772; weekdays, 8:30 A.M. to 5 P.M. ET. WEBSITE: www.cpsc.gov.

Waste Management

- **Earth 911** Locate disposal sites and household–hazardous-waste programs in your area. PHONE: 800-253-2687; 24 hours a day. WEBSITE: www.earth911.org.

Index

Credits

REAL SIMPLE

Managing Editor Kristin van Ogtrop

Editorial Development Director James Ireland Baker

Deputy Managing Editor Jacklyn Monk

Editorial Development Design Director Eva Spring

Editor Jaimee Zanzinger

Deputy Editor Rachel Hardage

Art Director Michele Walthers

Designers Catherine Hawthorn, Carolyn Veith Krienke

Editorial Assistant Nubia DuVall

Art Assistant Jennifer Klock

Copy Chief Nancy Negovetich **Copy Editor** Janet Kim

Research Chief Westry Green

Research Editors Carlos Greer, Ivette Manners

Contributing Editor Elizabeth Schatz Passarella

Photo Editor Naomi Nista

Editorial Production Manager Dominick Santise

Imaging Manager Steve Cadicamo

Assistant Imaging Manager Claudio Muller

Imaging Specialist Robert Pizaro

Imaging Coordinator Rey Delgado

TIME INC. HOME ENTERTAINMENT

Publisher Jim Childs

Vice President, Finance Vandana Patel

Executive Director, Business Development Suzanne Albert

Executive Director, Marketing Services Carol Pittard

Executive Director, Marketing Susan Hettleman

Publishing Director Megan Pearlman

Assistant General Counsel Simone Procas

Assistant Director, Special Sales Ilene Schreider

Senior Production Manager Susan Chodakiewicz

Editor, Brand Development Katie McHugh Malm

Associate Prepress Manager Alex Voznesenskiy

Associate Project Manager Stephanie Braga

Editorial Director Stephen Koepp

Senior Editor Roe D'Angelo

Copy Chief Rina Bander

Design Manager Anne-Michelle Gallero

Editorial Operations Gina Scauzillo

SPECIAL THANKS TO

Ben Ake, Amanda Armstrong, Katherine Barnet, Brad Beatson, Jeremy Biloon, Vanessa Boer, Ryan Bourquin, Leah Brown, Rose Cirrincione, Assu Etsubneh, Mariana Evans, Christine Font, Jean Forte, Kate Gleason, Hillary Hirsch, David Kahn, Aundrea King, Noirin Lucas, Amy Mangus, Kimberly Marshall, Nina Mistry, Kate Parker, Ashley Phillips, Dave Rozzelle, Matthew Ryan, Ricardo Santiago, Mary Sarro-Waite, Nykia Spradley, the Tarzian family, Adriana Tierno, Kristine Trevino.

SPECIAL THANKS TO THE FOLLOWING EXPERTS

Arm & Hammer; Randy Barr, My Home; Anthony Basilio Jr., DuPont Surfaces; Michael Berman, Lamps Plus; Jeff Bishop, Institute of Inspection, Cleaning, and Restoration Certification; Patricia Blick, the Fireplace Company; Dan Block, K and K Antique Restoration and Refinishing; Catherine Blomstrom, Catherine Blomstrom Carpentry; Steve Boorstein, www.clothing doctor.com; Brett Brenner, Electrical Safety Foundation International; BuildDirect; Lenora Campos, Toto USA; Bill Case, Gallow Restorations; Sattie Clark, Eleek Inc.; Richard Coch, the Joyce Theater; Jamie Columbus, Office Depot; Gene Cyranski, Sears Tower; Chris Davis, World Floor Covering Association; Hazel Davis, Waldorf-Astoria; Stacy DeBroff, www.momcentral.com; Michael Desiderio, Tavern on the Green; Randy Eades, Leather World Technologies; Forbo Flooring; Four Seasons Hotel Miami; Doug Fratz, Consumer Specialty Products Association; Craig Freeman, Turning Star Inc.; Christopher Gavigan, Healthy Child Healthy World; Deborah Gavito, Counter Restaurant; Geek Squad; General Electric; Gary and Roy Gold, Stain Rx; Joey Green, www.wackyuses.com; Neeraj Gupta, Service-Master Clean; Joseph Hallak Jr., Hallak Cleaners; Dr. Patricia Hametz, Morgan Stanley Children's Hospital of New York–Presbyterian; Max Harris, GreenFloors; Matthew Hittle, Ohio EPA Division of Solid and Infectious Waste Management; Linda Hopkins, American Cork Products; Anita Howard, National Wood Flooring Association; Frederick M. Hueston, National Training Center for Stone and Masonry Trades; Jim Ireland,

Credits (continued)

White Glove Elite; Bruce E. Johnson, DIY Network; Dale Kemery, U.S. Environmental Protection Agency; Yesmeen Khan, Library of Congress; Laurie Kilpatrick, *Miss Laurie's Smart Guide to House Cleaning;* Lynn Kimsey, University of California, Davis; Mary Kirkland, Kennedy Space Center; Allan Knight, Allan Knight Acrylic; Richard Frank Kulzer, Frank's Windows; Bill Lafield, Consumer Specialty Products Association; Steve Lovsteen, Oliver Twist Chimney Sweep; Cindy Mannes, National Pest Management Association; Teni Melidonian, Academy of Motion Picture Arts and Sciences; Maria Mergel, Washington Toxics Coalition; John Molla, Clean Tex; Sally Morse, Hunter Douglas; Keil Moss, Keil's Antiques and Moss Antiques; Marty O'Gorman, Frigidaire; Amy Olson, the Maids Home Services; Bill Ondratschek, Duraclean International; Dee Patel, Hermitage Hotel; Frank Prial, Beyer Blinder Belle Architects & Planners LLP; Deborah Racicot, Gotham Bar and Grill; Allen Rathey, www.housekeeping channel.com; Anne Reichman, www.earth911.com; Alicia Rockmore, Buttoned Up Inc.; Joseph Rubino, Lysol; Mag Ruffman, www.toolgirl.com; Sanford; Brian Sansoni, Soap and Detergent Association; Toby Saville, Dyson Laboratories; Michelle Shaeffer, Naturally Frugal Cleaning; Manon Slome, Chelsea Art Museum; Richard Smith, JRS Cleaners; Sarah Smock, Merry Maids; Mark Spencer, Sears Tower; R.J. Spomer, RJ Fine Woodworking; Staples; Tabitha Steinbock, Kohler; Claudia Sutherland; Meg Sutherland, Eco Friendly Flooring; Ruth Travis, Institute of Inspection, Cleaning, and Restoration Certification; Glenn Turner, Kennedy Center; Diane Van, United States Department of Agriculture Food Safety & Inspection Service; Schar Ward; Pamela Watts, Grand Sierra Resort and Casino; Robert L. Wolke; Michele Zelman, Armstrong Floor Products.

SPECIAL THANKS TO THE FOLLOWING COMPANIES

Aero (www.aerostudios.com) for furnishings; Blue Bench (www.bluebenchnyc.com) for child's bedroom furnishings and toys; Cath Kidston (www.cathkidston.com) for pillows; Chilewich (www.chilewich.com) for floor mats; C.O. Bigelow Chemists (www.bigelow chemist.com) for cosmetics and toiletries; Garnet Hill (www.garnethill.com) for bedding; Gracious Home (www.gracioushome.com) for cookware and cleaning products; Jonathan Adler (www.jonathanadler.com)

for home accessories; Restoration Hardware (www.restorationhardware.com) for bathroom textiles, accessories, and cleaning supplies; Seabrook Wallcoverings (www.seabrookwallpaper.com) for wallpaper; the Container Store (www.thecontainerstore.com) for organizational and office-supply products; Waterworks (www.waterworks.com) for bathroom accessories.

Photographs of supplies in Cleaning Kit and surfaces in Stains by Time Inc. Digital Studio.

Published by Real Simple Books, an imprint of Time Home Entertainment Inc., 1271 Avenue of the Americas, 6th floor, New York, NY 10020.
Real Simple is a trademark of Time Inc.

First Time Home Entertainment paperback edition October 2007 ISBN 13-digit: 978-1-933821-39-9
ISBN 10-digit: 1-933821-39-6
Printed in the U.S.A.

We welcome your comments and suggestions about Real Simple Books. Please write to us at: Real Simple Books, Attention: Book Editors, P.O. Box 11016, Des Moines, IA 50336-1016

If you would like to order any of our hardcover Collector's Edition books, please call us at 1-800-327-6388, Monday through Friday, 7 A.M. to 8 P.M., or Saturday, 7 A.M. to 6 P.M., Central Time.